Jayne Persico presents...

Kiln Formed Bracelets

D0521372

Wardell
PUBLICATIONS INC

Jayne Persico presents...
Kiln Formed Bracelets
is Copyright© 2005 by
Wardell Publications Inc.

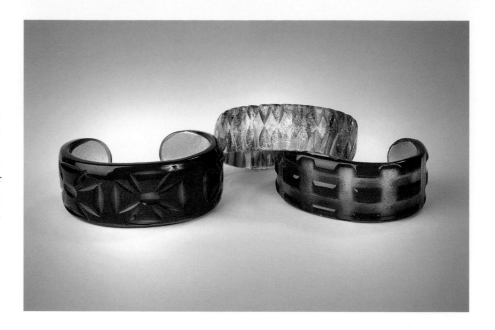

Cataloging in Publication Data

Persico, Jayne
    Jayne Persico presents... Kiln Formed Bracelets / Jayne Persico; text editor, Randy Wardell; jewelry design & fabrication, Jayne Persico; photography, Bill Reshetar Photography.

Includes index

ISBN-13: 978-0-919985-49-0
ISBN-10: 0-919985-49-1

    1. Glass fusing. I. Wardell, Randy A. (Randy Allan), 1954- II. Title. III. Title: Kiln Formed Bracelets.

NK5440.J48P473 2005   748.2'028   C2005-904816-6

Printed in Thailand by Phongwarin Printing Ltd.
Published simultaneously in Canada and USA
E-mail: info@wardellpublications.com
Website: www.wardellpublications.com

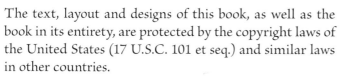

Jayne Persico presents...

Kiln Formed Bracelets

Author
Jayne Persico

Text Editor
Randy Wardell

Jewelry Design & Fabrication
Jayne Persico

Photography
Bill Reshetar Photography

Book Layout & Typography
Randy Wardell

Acknowledgements
My deepest appreciation to Dody Ottaviani for her wonderful assistance and support in both the studio and classroom but most especially for being my best friend. A special thanks to my studio staff; Tino, Anton, Ryan and Ross. Thanks and appreciation to following people and/or companies for all you do; Don McKinney, Nancy Roman, Bill Reidsema, Randy Wardell, Bill Reshetar, The Uroboros Glass Studios, Coatings by Sandberg, Waterford Crystal, Spectrum Glass Co., The Bullseye Glass Co, Aim Kilns, Gemini Saw Co. and The Glastar Corporation. And finally a very special thank you to my family for their love and support!

Published by

Wardell
PUBLICATIONS INC

To receive our electronic newsletter or to send suggestions please contact us
by E-mail: info@wardellpublications.com or visit our Website: www.wardellpublications.com

A Message from the Author

I've researched and experimented with a wide range of art glass techniques during the past thirty years. Fused glass connected with my love of jewelry design allowing me to blend my practical knowledge in both and venture into the field of art glass jewelry. I explored wire-wrapping and embellishment techniques before I began my experiments into the development of a unique process to create 'Kiln Formed Bracelets.' Eventually leading me to create a line of tools to enable others to form these bracelets in their own kilns.

The first kiln formed cane bracelet that the author made while she was still in the development stage of this unique process.

When the forming technique and tools were finished, I seized the opportunity to create an array of bracelet styles and designs. I soon began to wonder if I could find a way to blend and twist colors, to create intricate canes that I could then form into bracelets. Being a kiln former at heart I wanted to find a way to accomplish this in the kiln. My strong desire was my motivation and very soon I was successfully pulling beautiful canes that could be formed into stunning bracelets.

During the development period for each new process I found new inspirations just waiting to be explored. For instance, the casting process requires patience and involves several complicated steps to complete a bracelet. For me this challenge is most rewarding, however when conducting seminars I found that this was not always true with my students. They did want more texture in their work but had little desire to go through all the necessary stages to cast a bracelet. That directed me to the next advancement 'The Embossing System' - a technique that is quick and easy and creates a fabulous assortment of textures in glass.

My work in kiln formed bracelets has not only been personally gratifying it has also opened many doors for me to explore new possibilities. I was particularly delighted to be invited to experiment with cutting and faceting at the exclusive Waterford Crystal Factory in Ireland. The combination of American technology in color and dichroic glass along with the age old tradition of brilliant diamond wheel cut designs captured a rich effect of sparkling colors locked inside cut crystal encasements. What a thrill to be involved in an entirely new art form, one that has become my passion and is now an intricate part of my current work.

The creative process continues to flourish in my bracelets as well as my watches. The possibilities are endless and the development will never stop. For me kiln formed bracelets will always remain an important focus. As an artist and long-time instructor, it gives me great pleasure to share some of my bracelet making methods with you through this book. I hope that you will come away with new ideas that will lead you to your own personal exploration in glass. Thank you for allowing my creative journey to be a part of yours.

Jayne Persico

Author Contact Information

J. P. Glassworks Studio
50 North Vine Street,
Hazleton, PA 18201 USA
Email: info@jpglassworks.com
Website: www.jpglassworks.com

Table Of Contents

Bracelet Showcase Galleries

Introduction

What This Book Is About...and What It Isn't

My first book 'Innovative Adornments' was published in 2002. The subtitle of that book is 'An Introduction to Fused Glass & Wire Jewelry' and that is a pretty good description of what you will find. I covered all the basics starting from an in depth explanation of what fusing compatible glass is and what varieties you will find in the market. I discussed the assortment of glass tools that you will need from cutters & breakers all the way to grinders & diamond bladed saws. You will find information on various glass kilns and fusing accessories and a complete description of all the necessary wire wrapping tools.

The nearly 80 pages of instructions include basic glass scoring and breaking, plus fusing techniques for cabochons, pendants and other assorted components for jewelry creations. A good deal of the instruction focuses on the wire wrapping techniques that will enable and motivate you to create your very own Innovative Adornments!

I covered all the basics in that first book and that is why I did not include comprehensive instructions on those techniques in this book. Those basic procedures are extremely important, please do not assume that you can start your fused jewelry training with this book, without first having a fusing foundation. You really need to have a firm grasp on the fundamentals of glass fusing and have a working knowledge of jewelry making to enable you to successfully move to this more experienced level of kiln forming. In other words, you need to have 'been there and done that' before you jump into the 'hot firing' procedures presented in this book. The techniques in this book are not overly difficult but a little 'experience' will go a long way.

Kilns, Controls, Pyrometers, and Temperatures:

You will find several small portable kilns available on the market, these are sometimes referred to as 'tabletop' kilns. Most use ordinary household electrical current and do not require special wiring hook-ups. Each model has its own unique properties such as interior size, controls, loading profiles and other features (i.e. viewing window, side doors etc). They all can be used to fuse glass but only a couple can accommodate the kiln formed bracelet process. In order to successfully form a bracelet, a kiln must be top loading, the heating elements must be in the sidewalls and the lid must be completely removable.

Aim Kilns manufactures the portable kiln that I used for the projects in this book. It has an interior measurement of 8" x 8" wide x 4" deep (20.3 x 20.3 x 10.2 cm) that easily accommodates the bracelet forming mandrel. The side firing elements heat the kiln up rapidly and the controller is an infinite switch (rather than a step position switch) that provides finer control over the power selection. The removable center ring facilitates easy loading and the lid is also removable providing unrestricted access when it's time to manipulate the bracelet during the hot forming process.

All kilns are not created equal when it comes to temperature accuracy. Even the same models, manufactured by the same company, can be different. The 1st column in the chart below lists 6 critical firing stages that we need to know for the projects in this book. The 2nd column lists the conventionally accepted standard temperature for each stage (if taken with a precision pyrometer). The 3rd column illustrates the temperature range that you will typically find for that particular firing stage when viewing the analog pyrometer display on one of these tabletop kilns.

You will soon discover that I depend very much on visual monitoring during firing for the projects in this book. The uncertainty of accurate temperature readings, coupled with other variables during fusing such as glass color, project thickness, ramping & soaking times, etc., only serves to intensify the need for careful and frequent monitoring.

Every kiln has unique heating characteristics, so it's important to determine and record the pyrometer reading for each of the firing stages listed in the chart. In addition you'll want to know the controller position that will maintain a 'soaking' temperature for each of these stages. It will take a few firings to find the appropriate temperatures and kiln switch settings to maintain these various soaking temperatures for your particular kiln. Keep accurate records as you fire your projects to help you fine-tune your readings and settings. Once you have established those points of reference for your kiln, you will be set for as long as you own that kiln.

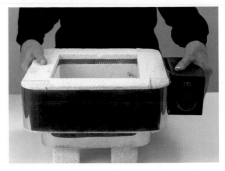

This photo shows the center ring being placed on the kiln base. The lid is completely removable and that allows unobstructed access to the inside of the kiln, making bracelet forming possible.

This kiln has an 'infinite' style kiln controller switch and an analog pyrometer readout gauge.

Firing Stage Description	Industry Standard	Typical Temperature Range for a Tabletop Kiln Analog Pyrometer	My Kiln's Temperature	My Controller Switch Position
Anneal Soak	960°F (516°C)	960°F (516°C) to 1025°F (552°C)		
Initial Slump	1250°F (677°C)	1250°F (677°C) to 1350°F (732°C)		
Fire Polish	1325°F (718°C)	1325°F (718°C) to 1425°F (774°C)		
Tack Fuse	1375°F (746°C)	1375°F (746°C) to 1475°F (802°C)		
Full Fuse	1450°F (788°C)	1450°F (788°C) to 1550°F (843°C)		
Embossing	1500°F (816°C)	1500°F (816°C) to 1600°F (871°C)		

Use this chart to record your kiln's pyrometer readings and controller switch position for the six critical firing stages. Make these determinations over several firings and write them down as you gain experience using your kiln.

Chapter 1 – Tools & Measurements

Bracelet Forming Tools & Supplies

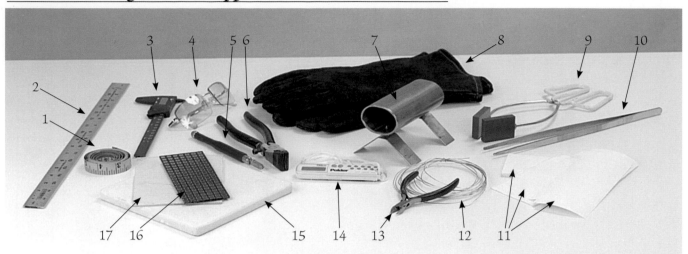

1. Fabric Measuring Tape
2. Steel Ruler (inches & metric)
3. Digital Caliper (see detail photo on page 9)
4. Safety Glasses
5. Glass Cutter
6. Glass Running Pliers (for breaking)
7. Bracelet Forming Mandrel
8. Hi-Temperature Kiln Gloves
9. Graphite Forming Tongs

10. Long Tweezers
11. Fiber Paper, (3 thicknesses)
12. Hi-Temperature (Nichrome) Wire
13. Flush Cutters (for wire cutting)
14. Digital Minute Timer
15. Mullite Kiln Shelf (with Kiln Wash)
16. Dichroic Patterned Fusing Glass
17. Clear Fusing Compatible Glass

Wire Wrapping Tools & Supplies

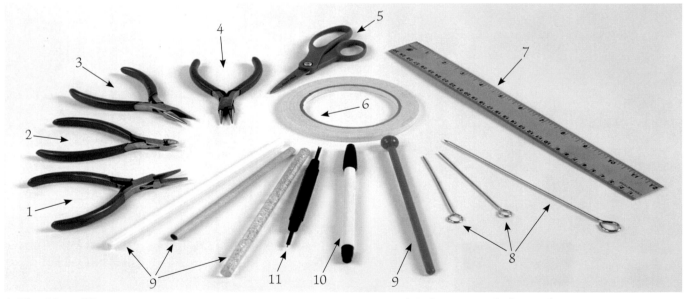

1. Flat Nose Pliers
2. Flush Cutters (wire cutters)
3. Needle Nose Pliers
4. Round Nose Pliers
5. Short Nosed Scissors
6. Quilter's Tape or Narrow Masking Tape

7. Metal Ruler - 12 inch (30 cm)
8. Metal Skewers - in assorted sizes
   3/64", 1/6", & 1/8" (1.2, 1.6, & 3.2 mm)
9. Dowels (to form loops and/or coils)
10. Marking Pen (fine point)
11. Watch Pin Tool (for watch band pins)

Jayne Persico presents...

Size Matters

Size is by far THE MOST IMPORTANT consideration when creating a glass bracelet. Glass is a rigid material that cannot be bent or reshaped as you could do with a metal bracelet, so it's essential to have a precision fit. Glass bracelets are sized using a 'cuff' style fit rather than the much looser 'bangle' style. We have created a set of easy to use charts (on pages 10 & 11) to enable you to determine the bracelet size based on a few simple measurements. Don't panic when you see the chart pages. You only need to find 2 numbers by connecting the rows and columns - it's as easy as finding the distance between 2 cities on a highway driving map.

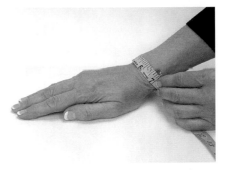

Measure the wrist around wrist bone.

Taking the Measurements

1. Use a fabric measuring tape to measure the wrist's circumference around the wrist bone (this is the bump on your wrist). It is important to be as precise as possible with this measurement. The tape measure should be snug but not too tight. Add 1/8" (3.2 mm) to this measurement for a normal fitting bracelet (you could add as much as 1/4" (6.4 mm) for a loose fitting bracelet). Write this resulting measurement in the space provided in row 'A' on the 'Measurement Data Form' below.

2. Next use a digital caliper to measure the thickness of your wrist - just above the wrist bone. This is the softer area on your wrist where these bracelets are normally placed. Make sure the calipers are quite snug! Write this measurement in the space provided in row 'B' on the 'Measurement Data Form.' This dimension will be the opening 'gap' size of your bracelet and is a key component for determining the bracelet blank size. For example, if two people have the same wrist circumference size but their wrist thickness measurements are different, the length of the bracelet blank will also be different.

Measure the thickness of your wrist.

3. Select 2 pieces of compatible fusing glass for your bracelet project. Stack these two layers of glass together and use the calipers to measure the total thickness. Place the result in line space 'D' of the 'Data Form.' Note: If you already have a pre-fused blank that still needs to be sized and fire polished you could caliper the actual pre-fused blank.

Measurement Data Form

Code	Description	Measurement	How to get it
A	Wrist Circumference		Measure around the wrist bone and add 1/8" (3.2 mm)
B	Wrist Thickness (Opening size)		Use a digital caliper to measure the soft area on wrist
C	Measurement from Chart 1		Use the measurements from line A & B and find the cross match number in Chart 1
D	Stacked Glass Thickness		Use a digital caliper to measure the thickness of stacked glass
E	Final Bracelet Blank Length (ready to form)		Use the measurements from line C & D and find the cross match number in Chart 2

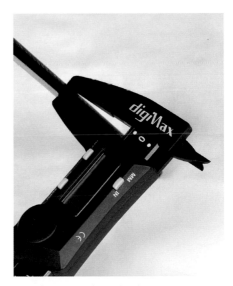

Use electronic digital calipers to measure the overall thickness of the stacked glass layers for your project.

Electronic digital calipers can measure in inches or metric with the touch of a button. This is a very handy tool that generates precision measurements for many areas of jewelry making.

Inch Sizing Charts

Chart 1: Find the 'Wrist Circumference' measurement (space 'A' from page 9) across the top row then find the 'Wrist Thickness' measurement (space 'B' from page 9) down the left column. Find the resulting cross match number by following along this column and row. Write this number in space 'C' of your Measurement data Form (page 9).

Chart 1	4 1/2	4 5/8	4 3/4	4 7/8	5	5 1/8	5 1/4	5 3/8	5 1/2	5 5/8	5 3/4	5 7/8	6	6 1/8
0.70	3 3/4	3 7/8	4	4 1/8	4 1/4	4 3/8	4 1/2	4 5/8	4 3/4	4 7/8	5	5 1/8	5 1/4	5 3/8
0.80	3 3/4	3 7/8	4	4 1/8	4 1/4	4 3/8	4 1/2	4 5/8	4 3/4	4 7/8	5	5 1/8	5 1/4	5 3/8
0.90	3 5/8	3 3/4	3 7/8	4	4 1/8	4 1/4	4 3/8	4 1/2	4 5/8	4 3/4	4 7/8	5	5 1/8	5 1/4
1.00	***	3 5/8	3 3/4	3 7/8	4	4 1/8	4 1/4	4 3/8	4 1/2	4 5/8	4 3/4	4 7/8	5	5 1/8
1.10	***	***	3 5/8	3 3/4	3 7/8	4	4 1/8	4 1/4	4 3/8	4 1/2	4 5/8	4 3/4	4 7/8	5
1.20	***	***	***	3 5/8	3 3/4	3 7/8	4	4 1/8	4 1/4	4 3/8	4 1/2	4 5/8	4 3/4	4 7/8
1.30	***	***	***	3 5/8	3 3/4	3 7/8	4	4 1/8	4 1/4	4 3/8	4 4/8	4 5/8	4 3/4	4 7/8
1.40	***	***	***	***	3 5/8	3 3/4	3 7/8	4	4 1/8	4 1/4	4 3/8	4 1/2	4 5/8	4 3/4
1.50	***	***	***	***	***	3 5/8	3 3/4	3 7/8	4	4 1/8	4 1/4	4 3/8	4 1/2	4 5/8
1.60	***	***	***	***	***	***	3 5/8	3 3/4	3 7/8	4	4 1/8	4 1/4	4 3/8	4 1/2
1.70	***	***	***	***	***	***	3 1/2	3 5/8	3 3/4	3 7/8	4	4 1/8	4 1/4	4 3/8

Chart 1	6 1/4	6 3/8	6 1/2	6 5/8	6 3/4	6 7/8	7	7 1/8	7 1/4	7 3/8	7 1/2	7 5/8	7 3/4	7 7/8
0.70	5 1/2	5 5/8	5 3/4	5 7/8	6	6 1/8	6 1/4	6 3/8	6 1/2	6 5/8	6 3/4	6 7/8	7	***
0.80	5 1/2	5 5/8	5 3/4	5 7/8	6	6 1/8	6 1/4	6 3/8	6 1/2	6 5/8	6 3/4	6 7/8	7	***
0.90	5 3/8	5 1/2	5 5/8	5 3/4	5 7/8	6	6 1/8	6 1/4	6 3/8	6 1/2	6 5/8	6 3/4	6 7/8	7
1.00	5 1/4	5 3/8	5 1/2	5 5/8	5 3/4	5 7/8	6	6 1/8	6 1/4	6 3/8	6 1/2	6 5/8	6 3/4	6 7/8
1.10	5 1/8	5 1/4	5 3/8	5 1/2	5 5/8	5 3/4	5 7/8	6	6 1/8	6 1/4	6 3/8	6 1/2	6 5/8	6 3/4
1.20	5	5 1/8	5 1/4	5 3/8	5 1/2	5 5/8	5 3/4	5 7/8	6	6 1/8	6 1/4	6 3/8	6 1/2	6 5/8
1.30	5	5 1/8	5 1/4	5 3/8	5 1/2	5 5/8	5 3/4	5 7/8	6	6 1/8	6 1/4	6 3/8	6 1/2	6 5/8
1.40	4 7/8	5	5 1/8	5 1/4	5 3/8	5 1/2	5 5/8	5 3/4	5 7/8	6	6 1/8	6 1/4	6 3/8	6 1/2
1.50	4 3/4	4 7/8	5	5 1/8	5 1/4	5 3/8	5 1/2	5 5/8	5 3/4	5 7/8	6	6 1/8	6 1/4	6 3/8
1.60	4 5/8	4 3/4	4 7/8	5	5 1/8	5 1/4	5 3/8	5 1/2	5 5/8	5 3/4	5 7/8	6	6 1/8	6 1/4
1.70	4 1/2	4 5/8	4 3/4	4 7/8	5	5 1/8	5 1/4	5 3/8	5 1/2	5 5/8	5 3/4	5 7/8	6	6 1/8

Chart 2: Find the 'Cross Match Number,' space 'C' in your Measurement data Form across the top row then find the 'Stacked Glass Thickness' (space 'D' from page 9) down the left column. Find the resulting cross match number by following along this column and row. Write this number in space 'E' of your Measurement data Form (page 9).

Chart 2	3 5/8	3 3/4	3 7/8	4	4 1/8	4 1/4	4 3/8	4 1/2	4 5/8	4 3/4	4 7/8	5	5 1/8	5 1/4
0.20	4	4 1/8	4 1/4	4 3/8	4 1/2	4 5/8	4 3/4	4 7/8	5	5 1/8	5 1/4	5 3/8	5 1/2	5 5/8
0.24	4 1/8	4 1/4	4 3/8	4 1/2	4 5/8	4 3/4	4 7/8	5	5 1/8	5 1/4	5 3/8	5 1/2	5 5/8	5 3/4
0.28	4 1/8	4 1/4	4 3/8	4 1/2	4 5/8	4 3/4	4 7/8	5	5 1/8	5 1/4	5 3/8	5 1/2	5 5/8	5 3/4
0.31	4 1/4	4 3/8	4 1/2	4 5/8	4 3/4	4 7/8	5	5 1/8	5 1/4	5 3/8	5 1/2	5 5/8	5 3/4	5 7/8
0.35	4 3/8	4 1/2	4 5/8	4 3/4	4 7/8	5	5 1/8	5 1/4	5 3/8	5 1/2	5 5/8	5 3/4	5 7/8	6
0.39	4 3/8	4 1/2	4 5/8	4 3/4	4 7/8	5	5 1/8	5 1/4	5 3/8	5 1/2	5 5/8	5 3/4	5 7/8	6
0.43	4 1/2	4 5/8	4 3/4	4 7/8	5	5 1/8	5 1/4	5 3/8	5 1/2	5 5/8	5 3/4	5 7/8	6	6 1/8
0.47	4 5/8	4 3/4	4 7/8	5	5 1/8	5 1/4	5 3/8	5 1/2	5 5/8	5 3/4	5 7/8	6	6 1/8	6 1/4
0.51	4 5/8	4 3/4	4 7/8	5	5 1/8	5 1/4	5 3/8	5 1/2	5 5/8	5 3/4	5 7/8	6	6 1/8	6 1/4

Chart 2	5 3/8	5 1/2	5 5/8	5 3/4	5 7/8	6	6 1/8	6 1/4	6 3/8	6 1/2	6 5/8	6 3/4	6 7/8	7
0.20	5 3/4	5 7/8	6	6 1/8	6 1/4	6 3/8	6 1/2	6 5/8	6 3/4	6 7/8	7	7 1/8	7 1/4	7 3/8
0.24	5 7/8	6	6 1/8	6 1/4	6 3/8	6 1/2	6 5/8	6 3/4	6 7/8	7	7 1/8	7 1/4	7 3/8	7 1/2
0.28	5 7/8	6	6 1/8	6 1/4	6 3/8	6 1/2	6 5/8	6 3/4	6 7/8	7	7 1/8	7 1/4	7 3/8	7 1/2
0.31	6	6 1/8	6 1/4	6 3/8	6 1/2	6 5/8	6 3/4	6 7/8	7	7 1/8	7 1/4	7 3/8	7 1/2	7 5/8
0.35	6 1/8	6 1/4	6 3/8	6 1/2	6 5/8	6 3/4	6 7/8	7	7 1/8	7 1/4	7 3/8	7 1/2	7 5/8	7 3/4
0.39	6 1/8	6 1/4	6 3/8	6 1/2	6 5/8	6 3/4	6 7/8	7	7 1/8	7 1/4	7 3/8	7 1/2	7 5/8	7 3/4
0.43	6 1/4	6 3/8	6 1/2	6 5/8	6 3/4	6 7/8	7	7 1/8	7 1/4	7 3/8	7 1/2	7 5/8	7 3/4	7 7/8
0.47	6 3/8	6 1/2	6 5/8	6 3/4	6 7/8	7	7 1/8	7 1/4	7 3/8	7 1/2	7 5/8	7 3/4	7 7/8	8
0.51	6 3/8	6 1/2	6 5/8	6 3/4	6 7/8	7	7 1/8	7 1/4	7 3/8	7 1/2	7 5/8	7 3/4	7 7/8	8

Metric Sizing Charts

Chart 1: Find the 'Wrist Circumference' measurement (space 'A' from page 9) across the top row then find the 'Wrist Thickness' measurement (space 'B' from page 9) down the left column. Find the resulting cross match number by following along this column and row. Write this number in space 'C' of your Measurement data Form (page 9).

Chart 1	11.3	11.7	12.0	12.3	12.7	13.0	13.3	13.7	14.0	14.3	14.7	15.0	15.3	15.7
1.75	9.6	9.9	10.3	10.6	10.9	11.2	11.6	11.9	12.2	12.6	12.9	13.2	13.6	13.9
2.00	9.3	9.7	10.0	10.3	10.7	11.0	11.3	11.7	12.0	12.3	12.7	13.0	13.3	13.7
2.25	9.1	9.4	9.8	10.1	10.4	10.7	11.1	11.4	11.7	12.1	12.4	12.7	13.1	13.4
2.50	***	9.2	9.5	9.8	10.2	10.5	10.8	11.2	11.5	11.8	12.2	12.5	12.8	13.2
2.75	***	8.9	9.3	9.6	9.9	10.2	10.6	10.9	11.2	11.6	11.9	12.2	12.6	12.9
3.00	***	***	9.0	9.3	9.7	10.0	10.3	10.7	11.0	11.3	11.7	12.0	12.3	12.7
3.25	***	***	***	9.1	9.4	9.7	10.1	10.4	10.7	11.1	11.4	11.7	12.1	12.4
3.50	***	***	***	***	9.2	9.5	9.8	10.2	10.5	10.8	11.2	11.5	11.8	12.2
3.75	***	***	***	***	8.9	9.2	9.6	9.9	10.2	10.6	10.9	11.2	11.6	11.9
4.00	***	***	***	***	***	9.0	9.3	9.7	10.0	10.3	10.7	11.0	11.3	11.7
4.25	***	***	***	***	***	***	9.1	9.4	9.7	10.1	10.4	10.7	11.1	11.4

Chart 1	16.0	16.3	16.7	17.0	17.3	17.7	18.0	18.3	18.7	19.0	19.3	19.7	20.0	20.3
1.75	14.3	14.6	14.9	15.2	15.6	15.9	16.2	16.6	16.9	17.2	17.6	17.9	***	***
2.00	14.0	14.3	14.7	15.0	15.3	15.7	16.0	16.3	16.7	17.0	17.3	17.7	18.0	***
2.25	13.8	14.1	14.4	14.7	15.1	15.4	15.7	16.1	16.4	16.7	17.1	17.4	17.7	18.1
2.50	13.5	13.8	14.2	14.5	14.8	15.2	15.5	15.8	16.2	16.5	16.8	17.2	17.5	17.8
2.75	13.3	13.6	13.9	14.2	14.6	14.9	15.2	15.6	15.9	16.2	16.6	16.9	17.2	17.6
3.00	13.0	13.3	13.7	14.0	14.3	14.7	15.0	15.3	15.7	16.0	16.3	16.7	17.0	17.3
3.25	12.8	13.1	13.4	13.7	14.1	14.4	14.7	15.1	15.4	15.7	16.1	16.4	16.7	17.1
3.50	12.5	12.8	13.2	13.5	13.8	14.2	14.5	14.8	15.2	15.5	15.8	16.2	16.5	16.8
3.75	12.3	12.6	12.9	13.2	13.6	13.9	14.2	14.6	14.9	15.2	15.6	15.9	16.2	16.6
4.00	12.0	12.3	12.7	13.0	13.3	13.7	14.0	14.3	14.7	15.0	15.3	15.7	16.0	16.3
4.25	11.8	12.1	12.4	12.7	13.1	13.4	13.7	14.1	14.4	14.7	15.1	15.4	15.7	16.1

Chart 2: Find the 'Cross Match Number', space 'C' in your Measurement data Form across the top row then find the 'Stacked Glass Thickness' (space 'D' from page 9) down the left column. Find the resulting cross match number by following along this column and row. Write this number in space 'E' of your Measurement data Form (page 9).

Chart 2	9.0	9.3	9.7	10.0	10.3	10.7	11.0	11.3	11.7	12.0	12.3	12.7	13.0	13.3
0.5	10.0	10.3	10.7	11.0	11.3	11.7	12.0	12.3	12.7	13.0	13.3	13.7	14.0	14.3
0.6	10.2	10.5	10.9	11.2	11.5	11.9	12.2	12.5	12.9	13.2	13.5	13.9	14.2	14.5
0.7	10.4	10.7	11.1	11.4	11.7	12.1	12.4	12.7	13.1	13.4	13.7	14.1	14.4	14.7
0.8	10.6	10.9	11.3	11.6	11.9	12.3	12.6	12.9	13.3	13.6	13.9	14.3	14.6	14.9
0.9	10.8	11.1	11.5	11.8	12.1	12.5	12.8	13.1	13.5	13.8	14.1	14.5	14.8	15.1
1.0	11.0	11.3	11.7	12.0	12.3	12.7	13.0	13.3	13.7	14.0	14.3	14.7	15.0	15.3
1.1	11.2	11.5	11.9	12.2	12.5	12.9	13.2	13.5	13.9	14.2	14.5	14.9	15.2	15.5
1.2	11.4	11.7	12.1	12.4	12.7	13.1	13.4	13.7	14.1	14.4	14.7	15.1	15.4	15.7
1.3	11.6	11.9	12.3	12.6	12.9	13.3	13.6	13.9	14.3	14.6	14.9	15.3	15.6	15.9

Chart 2	13.7	14.0	14.3	14.7	15.0	15.3	15.7	16.0	16.3	16.7	17.0	17.3	17.7	18.0
0.5	14.7	15.0	15.3	15.7	16.0	16.3	16.7	17.0	17.3	17.7	18.0	18.3	18.7	19.0
0.6	14.9	15.2	15.5	15.9	16.2	16.5	16.9	17.2	17.5	17.9	18.2	18.5	18.9	19.2
0.7	15.1	15.4	15.7	16.1	16.4	16.7	17.1	17.4	17.7	18.1	18.4	18.7	19.1	19.4
0.8	15.3	15.6	15.9	16.3	16.6	16.9	17.3	17.6	17.9	18.3	18.6	18.9	19.3	19.6
0.9	15.5	15.8	16.1	16.5	16.8	17.1	17.5	17.8	18.1	18.5	18.8	19.1	19.5	19.8
1.0	15.7	16.0	16.3	16.7	17.0	17.3	17.7	18.0	18.3	18.7	19.0	19.3	19.7	20.0
1.1	15.9	16.2	16.5	16.9	17.2	17.5	17.9	18.2	18.5	18.9	19.2	19.5	19.9	20.2
1.2	16.1	16.4	16.7	17.1	17.4	17.7	18.1	18.4	18.7	19.1	19.4	19.7	20.1	20.4
1.3	16.3	16.6	16.9	17.3	17.6	17.9	18.3	18.6	18.9	19.3	19.6	19.9	20.3	20.6

Chapter 2 - Creating The Bracelet Blank

Creating a basic bracelet blank is the first important step in mastering this kiln forming technique. Forming is so much more predictable when you have a uniform and well balanced blank to work with. Later, after you have some experience with the forming process, you can start to experiment with offset designs, molded shapes and even wheel cut patterns. For this first project we are going to create a basic 2 layer blank but we don't want to be boring so we'll use some patterned dichroic glass for the base layer, you simply can't go wrong with dichroic glass!

Tools & Equipment
- **Measuring & Preparation**
  steel ruler (inches & metric), marking pen (fine point)
- **Safety:** kiln gloves & safety glasses
- **Fusing:** kiln with pyrometer, kiln shelf, digital minute timer
- **Glass Cutting & Shaping:**
  glass cutter, breaking pliers, glass grinder

Materials
- **Glass Supplies:** clear fusing glass - standard thickness (large enough for a bracelet blank), dichroic patterned black fusing glass - standard thickness (large enough for a bracelet blank), glue (white craft) & applicator (toothpick)
- **Kiln Supplies:** kiln wash (hi-temp) & hake brush, fiber paper - 1/32" (0.8 mm) thickness

1. I recommend using two layers of standard thickness glass 1/8" (3 mm) for your first bracelet. I have selected a piece of black glass with a patterned dichroic surface for the base layer and a clear glass for the top layer of this project.

2. The base glass should be cut to the length that you calculated and recorded in space 'E' on page 9. The width is your choice, anywhere from 5/8" to 1" (1.6 cm to 2.5 cm). The top piece needs to be approximately 1/4" (6 mm) larger than the bottom piece (in both length and width) to allow the clear layer to slump down and around the bottom piece, to encase the edges (see photo and step 1 on page 40 for more details on this oversized top layer). Thoroughly clean both pieces of glass for your bracelet blank before placing them on the kiln shelf. Glue them together using a small dab of glue at the ends only.

3. The small tabletop kiln that I use consists of a base section, supported by four fire-brick blocks, a center ring that houses the heating elements and a removable lid section. This style of kiln allows me to conveniently position the glass on the kiln shelf before placing the center ring. Prepare a kiln shelf with 3 or 4 coats of kiln wash and allow it to dry completely (see page 45, step 1 for more information on applying kiln wash). Place the kiln shelf on the kiln base and then place the stacked glass blank assembly in the center of the shelf.

4. Carefully position the center ring section on the kiln base and then place the lid on top.

5. Turn the kiln control switch to the 'High' setting and fire the bracelet blank to the full fuse temperature of 1450°F (788°C) to 1550°F (843°C) - refer to page 7 for an explanation of the temperature range. A full fuse cycle will typically take from 30 to 40 minutes in the type of tabletop kiln shown in these photos. Set your digital minute timer for 25 minutes to remind yourself that it's time to begin visually monitoring the progress of the fuse. You can safely open the kiln to view the firing once the kiln temperature is above 1100°F (593°C). Remember to wear kiln gloves and safety glasses as you do this. When the 2 layers of glass are completely fused together and the edges are rounded the blank has reached full fuse. Turn the kiln off and let it cool to room temperature. Do not open the lid or vent the kiln during this critical cool down period.

6. Allow the kiln to cool sufficiently before removing the fused bracelet blank from kiln. Proper cool-down could take anywhere from 1 1/2 hours to 2 1/2 hours and varies from kiln to kiln. You must let the cool down happen in its own time, do not peek or try to speed up the cooling as this only invites trouble.

7. Next we'll do some cold working to refine the shape of the bracelet blank. I like to grind the edges and gently round the ends to ensure a comfortable fitting bracelet. Be careful not to grind off too much off the length. When you are finished grinding it must be the exact measurement that you determined and recorded on row 'E' of the Measurement Data Form (page 9).

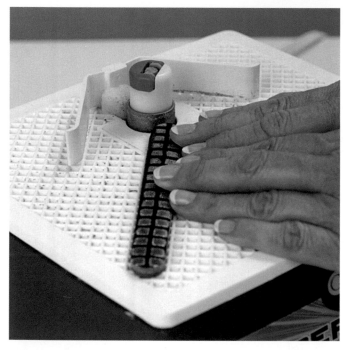

8. After cold working the blank must be placed back into the kiln to be 'fire polished' to restore the gloss to the areas that were cold worked. Use a finger-nail brush with soap and water to scrub and thoroughly clean the glass blank. Dry with a soft cloth and place it on a prepared kiln shelf, being careful not to touch the surface with your fingers. Turn the kiln control switch to the 'High' setting and fire the bracelet blank to the fire polishing temperature of 1325°F (718°C) to 1425°F (774°C). Set your digital minute timer for 20 minutes to remind yourself to visually monitor the progress. Put on your kiln gloves and safety glasses, lift the lid and carefully check the glass edges. The fire-polish is finished when they have a glossy and rounded-off appearance.

9. Turn the kiln off and allow it to cool sufficiently before removing the bracelet blank from the kiln. As you pick up the fired blank try to keep your fingers off the surface to reduce the need for cleaning before forming the bracelet. You are now ready to form the blank into a bracelet shape.

Tip: You can fire polish more than one bracelet blank at a time, provided there is enough room on the kiln shelf. It is important to leave at least 1/2" (1.3 cm) space between each of the blanks. The shelf size in this tabletop kiln could handle 3 or 4 blanks maximum.

Chapter 3 – Preparing The Bracelet Mandrel

Before we can actually place the glass blank on the mandrel and fire the kiln, we have to do some preparation work. Fiber paper is used to prevent the glass from sticking to the mandrel and also to resize the mandrel for an exact fit of the bracelet. Fiber paper has to be pre-fired (to remove the binders that can cause devitrification) before it can be placed on a mandrel.

Tools & Equipment
- **Measuring & Preparation** fabric measuring tape, steel ruler (inches & metric), marking pen (fine point), scissors
- **Safety:** kiln gloves & safety glasses
- **Fusing:** kiln with pyrometer, kiln shelf, digital minute timer
- **Forming & Manipulation:** bracelet forming mandrel, metal spatula
- **Jeweler's Tools:** flush cutters (wire cutters), needle nosed pliers

Materials
- **Kiln Supplies:** Thinfire™ paper or fiber paper in 1/32" (0.8 mm) thickness - several sheets, Nichrome wire (or copper wire)

Pre-Firing The Fiber Paper

1. I like to have a supply of pre-fired fiber paper on hand and ready to go before I start fusing blanks and forming bracelets. Happily, several pieces can be pre-fired at one time. There are a variety of fiber paper sizes available. The thinnest fiber paper (known as Thinfire™ paper) has a one-time use only (and does not require pre-firing). Thicker fiber paper such as 1/32" (0.8 mm) can be used more than once but it needs to be pre-fired to remove the binders that can cause devitrification (a white haze on the surface of the glass). You will also find fiber paper available in 1/8" (3.2 mm) thickness. This thicker size can be used as well but after pre-firing it has a tendency to crack when placed around the bracelet mandrel, that is why I recommend only the 1/32" (0.8 mm) thick paper for adjusting the mandrel size.

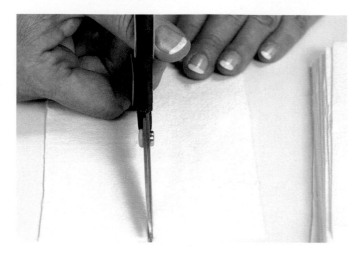

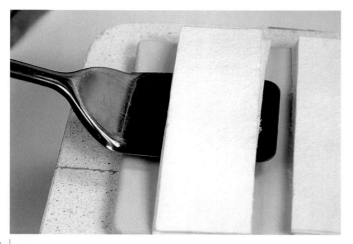

2. Use standard scissors to cut 6 to 16 pieces of fiber paper into strips that are about 3" X 6 1/2" (7.6 x 16.5 cm). You can combine assorted thicknesses of fiber paper in one firing if you're using them.

3. Find a well ventilated area to set-up your kiln. As the organic binder burns out it could set-off a smoke alarm, so it may be wise to use a fan to direct the fumes out an open window or somewhere they can dissipate. Assemble the kiln base, the center ring and place a kiln shelf inside. Position two stacks of fiber paper side-by-side, on the kiln shelf. Each stack could have anywhere from 3 to 8 sheets (depending on sheet thickness).

4. Vent the kiln by quarter-turning the lid to partly open all corners. Turn the control to 'High' and fire to approximately 1400°F (760°C). The fiber paper will turn brown at first and then back to white again, indicating that the binders have burned out.

5. When the burn-off is finished (no more smoke or smell) turn the kiln off and let it cool to room temperature.

6. Remove the kiln lid and center ring and set them aside. The fiber paper is rather delicate after it has been pre-fired and is easily damaged, use a kitchen spatula to carefully lift the fiber paper stacks and place them in zip-lock bags or a plastic sealer container for safe storage.

Tip: It will take a little longer for the very center of a large stack to fully cure. If you are pre-firing a full load, allow the kiln to soak (hold this temperature) for an additional 15 or 20 minutes at the 1400°F (760°C), then turn the kiln off and let it cool.

Jayne Persico presents...

Preparing & Sizing The Bracelet Mandrel

1. Ok, we're ready to select and dress the mandrel that we will use to shape our bracelet. Mandrels are available in three sizes: small - for wrists up to 6" (15 cm), medium/large - for wrists from 6" to 8" (15 to 20 cm) and extra-large (for wrist sizes larger than 8" (20 cm). Choose the mandrel size that corresponds to the 'A' row dimension you recorded in the Bracelet Measurement Data Form (page 9).

2. To ensure the bracelet fits comfortably on your wrist, the circumference of the mandrel needs to be exactly the same as dimension 'A' in your Data Form. Adjust the mandrel size by wrapping fiber paper around the center of the mandrel as needed. You may only need one layer of Thinfire™ paper (the thinnest available) or it could take several layers of the pre-fired fiber paper. Be sure to check the size with your fabric tape measure until the correct size is attained.

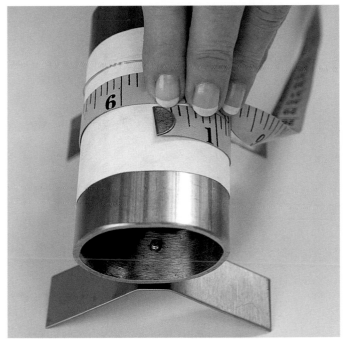

3. Secure the paper with a length of wire. You can use copper wire if you are only doing a single firing with this mandrel setup (copper wire softens and stretches after firing). However, if you will be using this size setup for several firings it's best to use hi-temperature Nichrome wire. Twist the wire securely on the bottom of the mandrel.

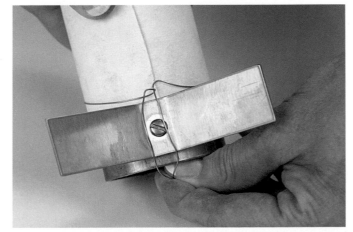

Chapter 4 - Kiln Forming the Bracelet

Tools & Equipment
- **Safety:** kiln gloves & safety glasses
- **Fusing:** kiln with pyrometer, digital minute timer
- **Forming & Manipulation:** bracelet forming mandrel, graphite forming tongs

Materials
- **Glass Supplies:** bracelet blank - sized, shaped and fire polished

You probably bought this book because you wanted to do what the title suggests, 'Kiln Formed Bracelets' so... here we go! This is the most exciting and interactive aspect of glass bracelet making. It also presents the most safety concerns. I can't stress enough just how careful and mindful you must be during this entire procedure. Two important things you need to remember (and do) are: 1. Never reach into the kiln until the power switch has been turned off. Those electric elements are hot - not just heat hot but electrically hot as well. You can get an electrical shock if you inadvertently touch an element, either directly or with a tool. 2. Always wear high temperature kiln gloves and safety glasses when you're working with a hot kiln. Sounds like common sense I know but you'd be surprised how many times I have to remind new students about this. If you get into the habit now - you won't be sorry later.

1. Setup the kiln base and place the center ring on the base (a kiln shelf is not necessary for this forming process). Position the mandrel in the kiln diagonally, making sure the probe for the thermal couple is at one end of the mandrel (see probe at top center of this photo) to ensure the probe won't interfere with the forming process.

2. Place your bracelet blank on the mandrel and adjust it until it is centered and balanced. The blank must be as close as possible to perpendicular (at a 90° angle) on the mandrel (see diagram on page 19, top right). If the angle is not correct the ends will not lineup after the bracelet is formed.

Jayne Persico presents...

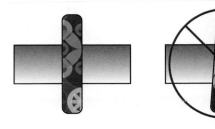

3. Place the lid on the kiln, being very careful that you do not disturb the glass blank. Turn the switch to the 'High' setting. Note: If your kiln is one of the smaller tabletop models that has a 6" (15 cm) interior, start the firing on the 'Medium' setting for 8 minutes and then turn it to 'High.' Set the timer for 15 minutes to remind you that the slumping process will happen in a shorter amount of time than when you're fusing. The bracelet should be ready to form in approximately 15-22 minutes.

4. When the kiln temperature reaches 1100°F (593°C) put on your kiln gloves & safety glasses and lift one side of the kiln lid a couple of inches to allow you to visually monitor the progress of the slump. The bracelet blank should still be straight (not bending) at this temperature. Close the lid for another minute or so, then open it again to take another peek, the ends may have started to slump by now. The temperature range for slumping is 1250°F (677°C) to 1350°F (732°C). If the slump has started, take note of the pyrometer reading and record it in the chart provided on page 7.

5. You are watching for the blank to soften enough to allow the ends to fall completely to the side - that is vertical to the kiln floor. It is critical to know precisely when the ends have fallen completely because at that moment you must close the lid and allow the kiln to soak at this temperature for another 45 to 75 seconds (length of time will depend on the glass color and thickness - see tip below). This additional soaking will soften the blank sufficiently, allowing it to be easily formed around the mandrel. However, you must be careful that the glass does not soften to the point where it stretches and alters the size of the finish bracelet. Use the soak time to get prepared for the manipulation process. Be sure you have your safety glasses and kiln gloves on and have the shaping tongs close by.

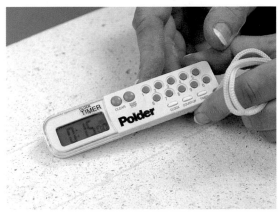

Tip: It's important to keep a very close watch on the firing. The 'initial slump' temperature occurs just as the bracelet blank first begins to soften. The pyrometer at that moment should be recorded in the chart on page 7, in the column 'My Kiln's Temperature.' Keep in mind that black glass and opalescent glass absorb heat faster than transparent glass and soften faster as a result. The pyrometer reading will be similar to that of other glass types but it will just take less time for dark glass to get to the optimum temperature. Conversely, thicker bracelets may need a little more time to absorb the heat before they can be successfully formed.

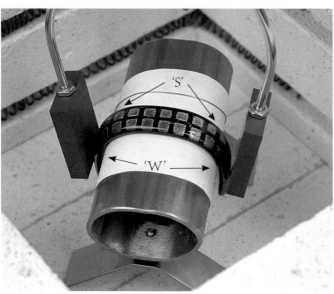

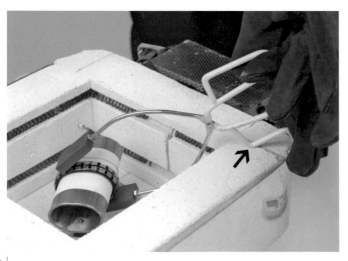

6. You may remember the adage that admonishes you to 'get out of your own way'. Well this is one of those times and is also the reason why it is important to hold the tongs using only your thumb and index fingers as shown in the photo. The remaining fingers should be clenched up and out of the way. If you don't get those fingers out of the way, they are going to get in the way as you form the bracelet and then it will be too late to change your hands. Your elbows need to be held up and away from your body. The grip and stance is going to feel strange and awkward at first but if you hold the tongs this way, the forming will be easy. So, study the photo (at left), put on your gloves and practice the grip a couple of times before you find yourself in the 'heat of the moment'.

7. Immediately after the soak period (from step 5), turn the kiln off, then remove the lid and set it aside. Pick up the tongs (holding them as instruct- ed) and start forming the bracelet by positioning the graphite pads of the tongs on the shoulder (position 'S' in the photo at left) of the bracelet. Now, make sure both graphite pads maintain constant contact with the glass as you carefully slide the pads down to the waist (position 'W' in the photo at left). Then apply a slight pressure to begin wrapping the lower section of the bracelet around the mandrel. Note: It is important to 'maintain constant contact' as you slide the tongs along the bracelet otherwise the bracelet could counteract on the mandrel and move off center.

8. Maintain the light contact and carefully rotate the tongs with a soft pressure and gentle guidance to snug one end of the bracelet around the bottom of the mandrel. Study the lower left photo and take special note of how the handles of my forming tongs are resting on the top frame of the kiln. I use the kiln edge as my guide, to ensure the bottom graphite pad is close to parallel with the bottom of the mandrel. This will guarantee a flush tuck on the inside of the bracelet.

Jayne Persico presents...

9. Repeat this same process on the other end of the bracelet. Remember to maintain that same constant contact with the graphite pads on the surface of the glass as you carefully rotate the tongs to the other end, making sure to once again use the edge of the kiln as your guide to get a flush tuck on the inside of the bracelet.

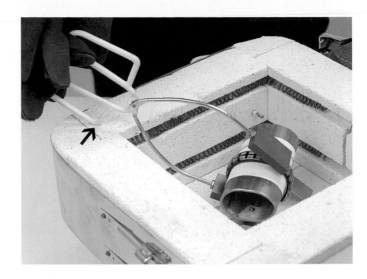

Tip: You'll have to work quickly while forming the bracelet. The glass will cool and become too stiff to manipulate within 15 to 20 seconds. It can be reheated if necessary however very often the glass will stretch as it reheats, deforming the shape and changing the size. It is best by far to practice the forming process until you have it down to an art and get it done in the first heating.

10. When you have completed the forming process, quickly replace the lid, wait 15 seconds or so and check the pyrometer, it should be reading somewhere in the 1000°F (540C) range. Plus or minus a few degrees is OK, but if it's substantially lower, you may have taken too long to manipulate the bracelet. In this case turn the kiln back onto the 'High' setting until it has recovered to 1000°F (540C).

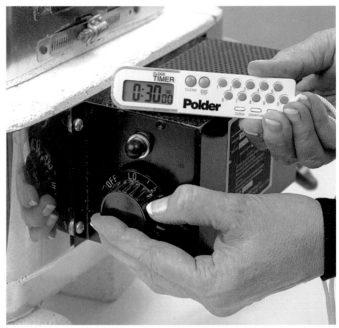

11. Adjust the controller switch to the anneal soak setting to maintain the optimum annealing temperature of 960°F (516°C) to 1025°F (552°C). A switch setting of Low, 1 or 2 should hold this 'soak' temperature in most tabletop kilns. An average bracelet of two layers of glass should be soaked (held) for approximately 30 minutes at the annealing temperature (set your timer as a reminder). If the bracelet is thicker it will need to be soaked for a longer period of time. After soaking, turn the kiln off and allow it to cool completely, this could take 2 to 3 hours or longer. Do not vent the kiln and don't yield to the temptation to take a peek.

12. When the kiln has cooled to room temperature, remove the lid, lift out the mandrel and carefully slide the bracelet off the end of the mandrel.

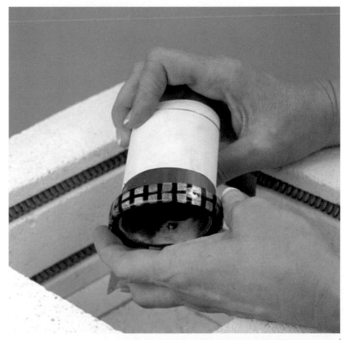

Bracelet Showcase Gallery

Chapter 5 - Making Adjustments

There are times when, in spite of your best efforts, a bracelet is not quite the correct size or perhaps the shape is slightly askew. It's relatively easy to make a minor adjustment to open or close the gap slightly but the overall size of the oval shape cannot be changed very much. That means a medium bracelet cannot be turned into a small bracelet or vice versa. Sometimes the bracelet may be the correct fit but the ends do not line up and one is higher than the other (they are skewed). This problem is also easy to fix.

Tools & Equipment
- **Safety:** kiln gloves & safety glasses
- **Fusing:** kiln with pyrometer, kiln shelf, digital minute timer
- **Forming & Manipulation:** graphite forming tongs

Materials
- **Glass Supplies:** Bracelet, formed and in need of a little adjustment
- **Kiln Supplies:** kiln wash (hi-temp) & hake brush

If the Bracelet Opening is Too Large

1. Prepare a kiln shelf with kiln wash (see page 45, step 1 for kiln wash instructions). Measure and mark the correct opening size directly on the kiln wash using a pencil. Remember that the 'B' dimension from your Bracelet Measurement Data Form on page 9 is the correct opening size. Place the bracelet on the shelf with opening centered directly over the pencil marks. Close the kiln, turn it to the 'High' setting and set the minute timer for 10 minutes. While you're waiting, put your safety glasses and kiln gloves on and make sure the shaping tongs are close by (remember to use the same grip on the tongs as described in step 6 on page 20).

2. When the pyrometer reading is 1150°F (566°C), turn the kiln off and remove the lid. Pick up the tongs and place the graphite pads on the outside of the bracelet and squeeze VERY GENTLY to close the bracelet until the ends match the pencil marks you made. If the glass is too stiff and will not move at this temperature, replace the lid, turn the kiln back on and let the temperature rise to 1175°F (635°C) and try again. If it is still too stiff add 25°F (14°) and try again, if necessary add another 25°F (14°C) until you are able to adjust the glass opening size. You must be very attentive, if you let the kiln get too hot the sides of the bracelet will collapse - and it gets too hot surprisingly quickly. It may take a few reheat-up trials until you determine the exact temperature reading that is best in your kiln for this process.

3. When you have successfully completed the resizing, replace the lid and adjust the kiln control switch to the anneal soak setting you have determined for your kiln (see page 7) and allow the bracelet to soak in the anneal range of 960°F (516°C) to 1025°F (552°C) for 30 minutes. When the anneal soak is finished, turn the kiln off and let it cool to room temperature. Do not vent or open the lid.

If the Bracelet Opening is Too Small

1. Repeat the previous step one (on page 24), laying the bracelet just slightly to the inside of the marks, so you can easily see them. Turn on the kiln, set the timer and get your glasses and gloves ready.

2. When the pyrometer reading is 1150°F (566°C), turn the kiln off and remove the lid. Pick up the tongs and place the graphite pads on the inside of the bracelet and pull VERY GENTLY on the tongs to open the bracelet until the ends match the pencil marks you made. As in step 2, on page 24, if the glass is too stiff and will not move, turn the kiln back on and let the temperature rise to 1175°F (635°C) and try again. If it is still too stiff add 25°F (14°) and try again, if necessary add another 25°F (14°C) until you are able to adjust the glass opening size.

3. When you are satisfied with the resizing, replace the lid and adjust the kiln control switch to the anneal soak setting (see step 3 above) and allow it to soak for 30 minutes (set your timer as a reminder). When the anneal soak is finished, turn the kiln off and let it cool to room temperature. Do not vent or open the lid.

If The Bracelet Opening Is Uneven (ends are skewed)

1. Prepare a kiln shelf with kiln wash. Lay the bracelet in the center of the kiln shelf, close the kiln, turn it to the 'High' setting and set the timer for 10 minutes. You will need to visually monitor the progress for this adjustment. You should wear your kiln gloves and safety glasses while monitoring but you won't need the graphite tongs.

2. This process will take less time than the resizing because gravity will be at work to bring the ends into line as soon as the temperature is correct. After the 10 minutes put on your kiln gloves and glasses and lift the lid to take a peek. By now, the higher side of the bracelet may have begun to slump down to the shelf. If it hasn't fallen completely flat to the shelf, close the lid for another minute or so and take another peek. Continue to monitor it until you are satisfied that the ends are even again - but you must be attentive! It is really easy to let it heat too much, causing the bracelet to collapse.

3. When you are happy with the adjustment, vent the kiln to 1000°F (535°C) then close the lid and adjust the kiln control switch to the anneal soak setting (see step 3 at top of this page) and allow it to soak for 30 minutes (set your timer as a reminder). When the annealing cycle is finished, turn the kiln off and let cool to room temperature. Do not vent.

Jaune Persico prese

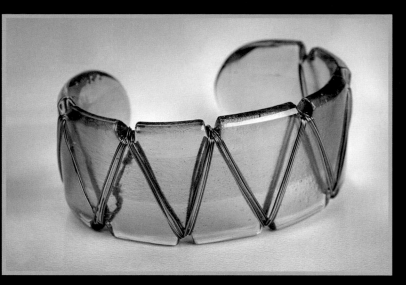

Chapter 6 – Notched Wire Wrapped Bracelets

Tools & Equipment
- **Measuring & Preparation** steel ruler (inches & metric), marking pen (fine point)
- **Safety:** kiln gloves & safety glasses
- **Fusing:** kiln with pyrometer, kiln shelf, digital minute timer
- **Glass Cutting & Shaping:** glass cutter, breaking pliers, glass grinder, diamond blade glass saw
- **Jeweler's Tools:** flush cutters (wire cutters), needle nosed pliers

Materials
- **Glass Supplies:** bracelet blank - fused, sized and shaped but not fire polished
- **Jewelry Supplies:** glass seed-beads - size 8/0 (3 mm), 5 ft (1.5 m) length of 24, 26 or 28 gauge round soft wire (could be, colored jewelry wire, sterling silver wire or gold filled wire)
- **Kiln Supplies:** kiln wash (hi-temp) & hake brush, pre-fired fiber paper - 1/32" (0.8 mm) thickness, Nichrome wire (or copper wire)

The instructions prior to this chapter provide the basic steps for creating and forming a bracelet using the 'direct manipulation method' that I have developed and refined over the years. I encourage you to create at leaset one or two bracelets with a simple basic design, before attempting one that uses the decorations and embellishments that we will add in the next few chapters. Precise setup and timing is everything when making these bracelets and it is so much better to learn the process by making a simple 2-layer bracelet.

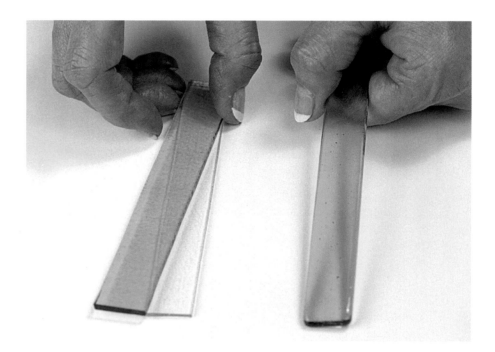

Create A Notched Bracelet

1. Make a 2-layer bracelet blank following steps 1 to 6 in Chapter 2 on pages 12 to 14. Remember to use the dimensions you calculated and recorded on your 'Measurement Data Form.' The photo above shows the bottom blue layer and the top clear layer before firing (at left) and the finished bracelet blank (at right) prior to notching and fire polishing. You can actually make 3 or 4 blanks in a single firing, provided the blanks are more or less the same (size, # of layers). The color combinations can be different but remember dark (especially black) glass heats up more quickly than lighter colors, so it's best if the base glasses have a comparable color-depth range.

2. Next we'll cold work the blank to refine the shape and add some decorative notches. Grind the edges and gently round the ends (but don't grind too much, remember it must be the exact measurement from row 'E' of your Measurement Data Form (page 9).

3. Use a ruler and a marking pen to evenly space out the locations for the notches. Mark one side first, then evenly stager the notches on the opposite side. Use a rigid wire-type diamond blade glass saw to cut the notches approximately 1/8" (3.2 mm) deep into the blank. It is important to try to make all notches the same depth.

4. After grinding and notching, the blank must be placed back into the kiln to be 'fire polished' (see basic bracelet, steps 8 & 9 on page 14). Remember to thoroughly clean the glass blank and place it on a prepared kiln shelf, being careful to not touch the surface with your fingers. When the edges appear to be glossy, the fire-polish is finished. Turn the kiln off and allow it to cool before removing the bracelet blank.

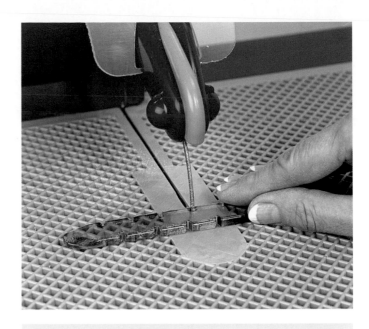

Tip: Just as you can fire polish 3 or 4 blanks in a single firing (see tip on page 14) you can also full fuse 3 or 4 blanks at one time. It is important to leave at least 1/2" (1.3 cm) space between the blanks. When firing several blanks at once it is advisable to run an annealing soak cycle for 30 minutes (refer to temperature chart on page 7).

5. The notched and fire-polished blank is now ready to be formed into the bracelet shape. Follow the steps in Chapter 3, page 15 to 17 to prepare the mandrel. Be sure the blank is clean before placing and centering it on the mandrel inside the kiln.

6. Kiln form the bracelet following the steps in Chapter 4, page 18 to 21. After forming, be sure to run an annealing soak cycle for 30 minutes (refer to temperature chart on page 7). After soaking, turn the kiln off and allow it to cool to room temperature. Do not vent or open the lid.

Wire Wrapping the Notched Bracelet

1. You will need approximately 5 feet (1.5 m) of round soft wire. I am using a 26-gauge silver decorative wire to add interest and hold the colored seed-beads. Decorative wire is available in gold, silver plus several other colors. You could choose a color that would compliment both the bracelet and the beads. I prefer to use 26-gauge wire because it is fine enough that it will lay flat on the inside of the bracelet and will not irritate your wrist.

2. Start the wire wrapping by placing one end of the wire on the inside of the bracelet near the center and hold it there with your thumb.

3. Wrap the wire through the last notch (the one that is closest to the end of the bracelet) and around the front (top) of the bracelet. Bring the wire to the back by laying it through the last notch on the opposite side. The last two notches on one end should now have wire through them. This will secure the wire for the time being.

4. Now continue to wrap the wire, coiling it around the bracelet and weaving it through the notches - first forward one notch then back one notch, forward again and then back - to create a distinctive "V" pattern on the surface of the bracelet (this is much easier to do than it sounds).

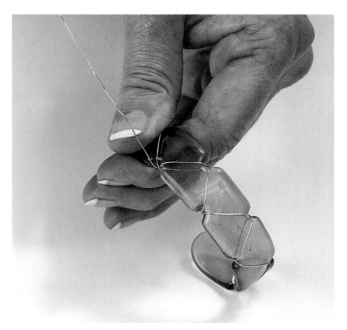

Jayne Persico presents...

5. Take a moment to inspect the wire pattern on the surface of the bracelet. Is the "V" pattern consistent on the front and back side?

6. For the next step we will double back on the bracelet and continue wrapping the wire, however this time we will place beads on the wire. Thread 3 or 4 beads onto the wire. The actual quantity is up to you, use enough to fit across the top surface of the bracelet. Wrap the wire with the beads strung on it across the top of the bracelet and into the notch on the opposite side. Continue to wrap it across the underside and coil it back up to the front, add more beads and continue wrapping and adding beads until you have reached the other end.

7. Check your work to make sure each row has the same number and combination of beads. When you're satisfied that it is the way you want it, wrap the final end of the wire under and around a group of wires on the inside. Use your needle nose pliers to pull the wire tight, then thread it through again, pull it tight, until you have wrapped it 4 to 5 times to form a coil.

8. After the coil is wrapped trim the wire end with the flush cutters as close as possible to the coil. Make sure this coil-knot is neat then use your needle nose pliers to tuck the wire end down and under (so it won't poke into your wrist) and finish it with tight pinch of the pliers.

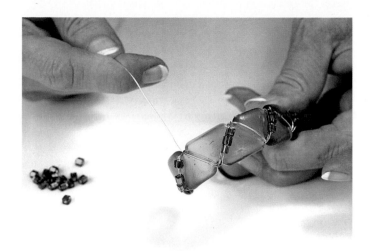

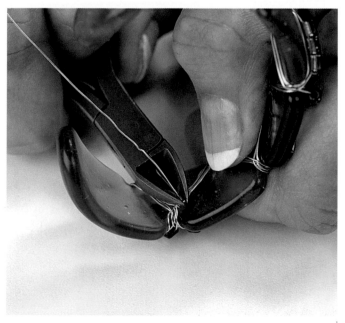

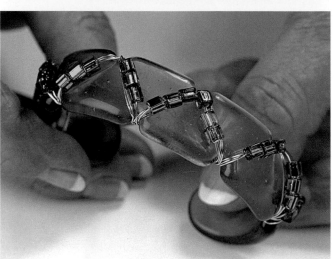

9. The last step is to secure the end of the wire where you started the wrapping. It will now be under several groups of wires on the inside. Use your needle nose pliers to slide this wire free, so that it can be secured in the same manner as the ending wire (follow steps 7 and 8 on page 31).

10. Take a moment to admire your finished bracelet and let your mind contemplate the possibilities for your next notched and wire wrapped bracelet.

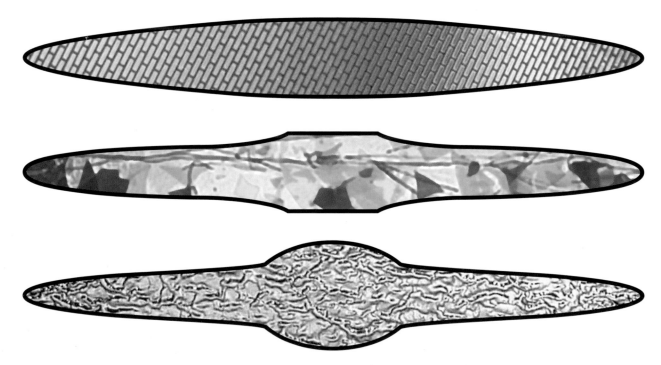

With a little imagination (and a diamond blade glass saw) you could easily alter the basic blank shape for a bracelet to create an interesting design. This illustration presents 3 examples of simple shapes that are possible. These shapes may not be suitable for notching and wire wrapping but they could be enhanced using pattern bar slices (see page 62) or embossing (see page 34).

Jayne Persico presents...

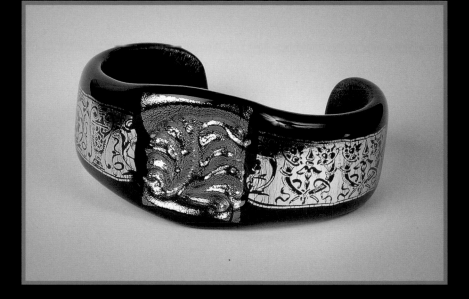

Chapter 7 – Single Embossed Medallion Bracelet

When glass is heated to just the right temperature it can be shaped, twisted, marked and manipulated in multiple ways, using a variety of tools. This chapter will explain how you can use an embossing process to imprint a decorative pattern directly into the surface of heat-softened glass. The procedure is not complicated but produces an art piece with an intricate and extraordinary sculptural effect.

Tools & Equipment
- **Measuring & Preparation**
  steel ruler (inches & metric), marking pen (fine point)
- **Safety:** kiln gloves & glasses
- **Fusing:** kiln with pyrometer, kiln shelf, minute timer
- **Glass Cutting & Shaping:** glass cutter, breaking pliers, glass grinder
- **Forming & Manipulation:** bracelet forming mandrel, graphite forming tongs, bronze embossing stamps, single embossing handle, metal tray

Materials
- **Glass Supplies:** black fusing glass - standard thickness (large enough for 2 layers of bracelet blanks), dichroic fusing on clear glass- standard or thin thickness (large enough for the bracelet center), glue (white craft) & applicator (toothpick)
- **Kiln Supplies:** pre-fired fiber paper - 1/32" (0.8 mm) thickness, Nichrome wire (or copper wire)

Embossing Tools & Supplies:

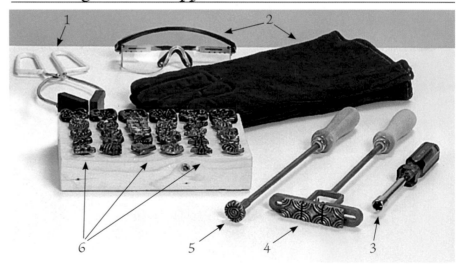

1. Graphite Forming Tongs
2. Safety Glasses & Kiln Gloves
3. Nut Driver (for embossing stamps)
4. Multi-Embossing Press Handle
5. Single-Embossing Press Handle
6. Bronze Embossing Stamps (assorted designs)

1. For this project I am using two layers of black glass along with a small rectangle of dichroic glass (also on black) for the center accent. The temperature and soaking times needed for successful embossing offers a distinct advantage. It is not necessary to prefuse, shape & grind to size, then fire polish the bracelet blank. All these steps, plus the embossing step, can be completed in one firing! However, to pull this off successfully it is crucial to be precise when measuring and shaping the glass blank components. In addition the firing temperatures and times are extremely critical, as over firing can easily expand the size. So be alert and attentive to what you're doing and you will reap the bonus of creating an embossed blank in one firing.

2. The top layer of glass must be cut to the exact length of dimension 'E' from your Bracelet Data form (page 9) and the width should be 3/4" (2 cm). The bottom layer needs to be slightly smaller, about 1/4" (6 mm) in both length and width. The picture shows the layers in reverse (bottom layer is on top); notice that there is approximately 1/8" (3 mm) showing all around the bottom layer. Now cut a piece of dichroic glass 3/4" (2 cm) x 1" (2.5 cm). Use a grinder to put a smooth edge and nicely rounded ends on the bottom layers and make sure the top layer (the larger component) is precisely the same length as dimension 'E.'

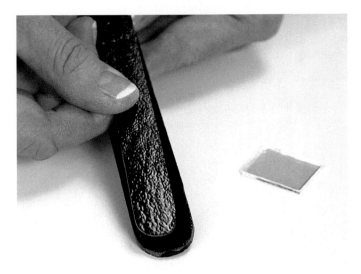

3. Place two SMALL dabs of white glue on the underside of the top layer (at the ends only - never in the center) and press the bottom layer into the glue to temporarily hold the two layers of glass together until they are fused.

4. Lay the blank assembly right side up on your worktable. Place a small dab of white glue on the back corners of the dichroic glass then position and secure it to the center of the blank. This third layer of glass will fuse into the bracelet blank and cause the center to bulge slightly due to the extra volume created by the smaller piece of dichroic glass. Take a look at the full fused blank in the photo on page 36, bottom left and you can clearly see this bulge effect. This is a particularly effective design element especially since we will be adding an embossed medallion in this bulge area.

5. Setup the kiln base and kiln shelf then lay a piece of 1/32" (0.8 mm) pre-fired fiber paper on the kiln shelf. This is one of those instances where you must use fiber paper on the shelf to prevent the very hot glass from sticking to the shelf wash.

6. Lay the blank assembly in the center of the fiber paper. If the blank doesn't fit across the shelf, you may have to turn it (and the fiber paper) diagonally, corner to corner. Place the center ring on the kiln base and close the lid. Turn the kiln to the highest setting and set your timer for 30 minutes.

7. While we're waiting for the blank to get up to temperature, we'll setup the embossing tool. Select a single bronze embossing stamp and screw it onto the single press handle. It is not necessary to coat the embossing stamp with a separator or kiln wash for this quick technique. It will not stick to the glass as long as the bronze is used when it's cool (at or near room temperature). Not surprisingly this means that if you intend to do more than one pressing in succession, the embossing stamp must be cooled between uses.

8. The optimal embossing temperature is approximately 1500°F (816°C) to 1600°F (871°C). If you know the exact full fuse temperature that works in your kiln, your could add 50°F (28°C) to that temperature.

9. When your kiln is close to the correct temperature, turn the infinite switch down one or two notches to a setting that will maintain a soak at this temperature. Once again a visual inspection is the best test, so put on your gloves and glasses, lift the lid a couple of inches and take a peek. You're looking for all layers to be fused together flat and the edges should be rounded. Be patient but also be careful that the temperature does not rise above the optimal embossing temperature because the glass will become too soft to emboss, causing thin areas and spiking on the outer edges of the bracelet. In addition the blank could spread out, making it too large for a proper fit after forming on the mandrel.

10. When the blank is ready to emboss, put on your kiln gloves and safety glasses, turn off the kiln (very important), remove the kiln lid and set it aside. Pick up the embossing tool (be sure to hold it by the wooden handle only, the metal rod will get hot quickly and you can burn your hand even through the gloves) and press it straight down into the center of the dichroic section in the bracelet. As you press you will feel the embossing stamp sink into the softened glass. Rock the handle from side to side and from front to back to fully impress the stamp design into the glass. The entire stamping process should take no more than 5 seconds.

Tip: If the glass was not hot enough and the embossed image is not crisp, replace the lid and soak it at the embossing temperature for a little longer, then try it again. The faint image that might be remaining on the glass from your first attempt will disappear when you emboss it again (remember to cool the embossing stamp to prevent sticking).

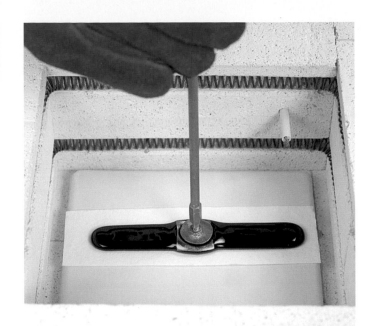

11. Remove the embossing tool and place it on a heat proof surface. Replace the kiln lid and adjust the switch to the anneal soak setting to maintain the annealing temperature of 960°F (516°C) to 1025°F (552°C) for 45 minutes. After soaking turn the kiln off and let it cool. Do not vent.

12. The final step is to form the blank on the mandrel. An embossed bracelet has several levels of thickness in the embossed design area. For this reason an embossed bracelet blank must be heated and cooled more slowly than a simple 2 layer bracelet, to prevent the glass from breaking. Prepare the mandrel as described in Chapter 3, pages 17. Place the embossed bracelet on the mandrel and turn the kiln to the 'Low' setting for 8 minutes. Then turn the kiln up to the Medium setting until it has reached 900°F (482°C). You can now safely turn the kiln onto the 'High' setting until it has reached the forming temperature range of 1250°F (677°C) to 1350°F (732°C). Follow the instructions in Chapter 4, steps 4-11 on pages 19 to 21. Anneal soak time for this embossed bracelet should be 45 minutes. Let cool to room temperature and do not vent during this time.

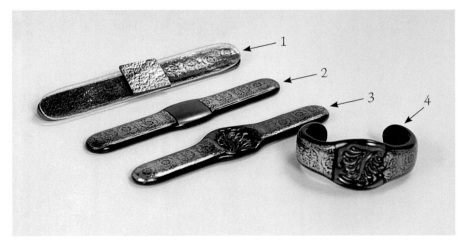

This photo shows the four stages of a single embossed bracelet. 1. Glass Cut and Shaped; 2. Fused and Fire-polished Blank; 3. Embossed Blank; 4. Formed & Finished Bracelet. Note: If you follow the process as presented in this chapter you will not have to actually create the stage #2 fire polished blank as shown here.

Bracelet Showcase Gallery

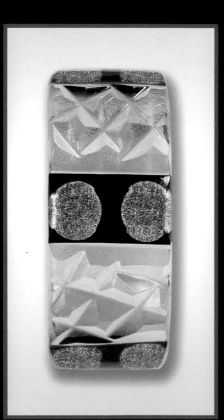

Chapter 8 – Multi Embossed Medallion Bracelet

We will make this multi embossed medallion bracelet using only two layers of glass. Just as we did in Chapter 7 we are going to fuse the bracelet blank and emboss it in a single kiln firing. Let me remind you that it is crucial to be precise when measuring and shaping the glass blank components.

Tools & Equipment
- **Measuring & Preparation:** steel ruler (inches & metric), marking pen (fine point)
- **Safety:** kiln gloves & glasses
- **Fusing:** kiln with pyrometer, kiln shelf, minute timer
- **Glass Cutting & Shaping:** glass cutter, breaking pliers, glass grinder
- **Forming & Manipulation:** bracelet forming mandrel, graphite forming tongs, bronze embossing stamps, multi-embossing press handle, nut driver (for embossing stamps)

Materials
- **Glass Supplies:** black fusing glass - standard thickness (large enough for a bracelet blank), dichroic on clear fusing glass - standard thickness (large enough for a bracelet blank), glue (white craft) & applicator (toothpick)
- **Kiln Supplies:** pre-fired fiber paper - 1/32" (0.8 mm) thickness, Nichrome wire (or copper wire)

1. The top layer of glass is clear dichroic cut to the exact length of dimension 'E' from your Bracelet Data form (page 9) and the width is 3/4" (2 cm). The bottom layer is cut from black glass and needs to be approximately 1/4" (6 mm) smaller in both length and width. For this picture we placed the bottom layer (black glass) on top and you can see there is about 1/8" (3 mm) of the clear dichroic glass showing all around the black glass. Use a grinder to smooth the edges and round the ends of both layers. After grinding, be sure to measure the top layer (the larger component) to ensure it is the same length as dimension 'E.' Make sure the dichroic coating is on the top side of the bracelet blank. Place two petite dabs of white glue on the underside (non-dichroic side) of the top layer and place the bottom layer on the glue to secure the layers.

2. Setup the kiln base and kiln shelf and lay a piece of pre-fired fiber paper on the kiln shelf. Mark the embosser position on the fiber paper (see tip below) then center the blank over these marks on the fiber paper. If your bracelet blank is a larger size, it may be necessary to turn the blank and fiber paper diagonally on the shelf.

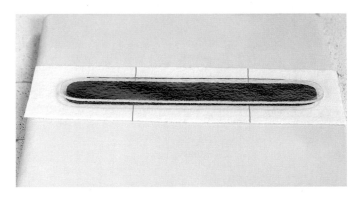

3. Place the center ring on the kiln base and close the lid. Turn the kiln to the highest setting and set your timer for 30 minutes.

4. Take those 30 minutes to setup your embossing tool. Select 3 of the bronze embossing stamps and secure them onto the multi-press handle. Use lock washers and nuts for the 2 outside embossing stamps and use a lock washer and wing nut for the center stamp pad.

5. Tighten the outside pads with the nut driver and firmly finger tighten the center wing nut to prevent the embossing stamps from turning and shifting when you impress the hot glass. It is not necessary to coat the stamps with a separator, they will not stick as long as the bronze is cool when it's pressed into the hot glass.

Tip: Centering the embossing stamp over a hot bracelet blank can be a tricky operation. Sometimes the blank has a built-in center target for the embossing stamp (i.e. the dichroic piece in chapter 7, page 36). However when the blank has a consistent color or design, it is next to impossible to hit the center in the heat of the moment. Remedy this by creating a target on the fiber paper or on the kiln shelf (or both) to indicate center. Place the embossing handle (either the multi-handle or the single handle with a bronze stamp attached) on the fiber paper and mark a pencil line at both ends. Then take away the handle and extend the lines all the way across the paper. Lay the bracelet blank on the paper, making sure the overhang on each end of the blank is the same (use a ruler if necessary). Now when you're ready to emboss, all you have to do is keep the ends of the embosser between the lines and you will know the image is centered in the bracelet.

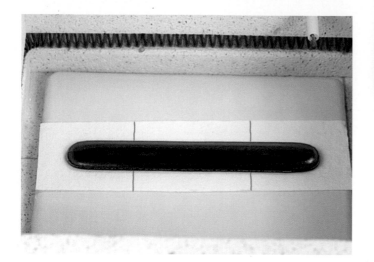

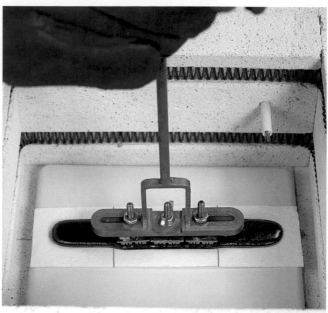

6. Review Chapter 7, steps 8 and 9 (on page 36) for details on attaining the optimum embossing temperature for the glass blank. When you think it's close, put on your gloves and glasses and lift the lid a couple of inches. You're looking for the layers to be fused flat with nicely rounded edges.

7. When you are satisfied that the blank is ready put on your gloves and glasses, turn off the kiln, remove the kiln lid and pick up the embossing tool (be sure to hold it by the wooden handle only). Position it over the center of the bracelet, line it up with the pencil marks then press straight down into the softened glass. Rock the handle from side to side and from front to back to fully impress the stamp design into the glass.

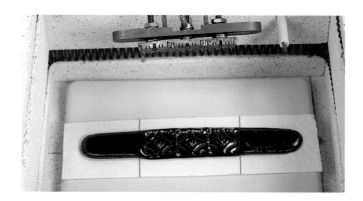

8. Remove the embossing tool and place it on a heat proof surface. Take a quick look at the embossed design, if it is not to your liking you can reheat and try again (see Tip on page 37). Replace the kiln lid and adjust the switch to the anneal soak setting to maintain the annealing temperature of 960°F (516°C) to 1025°F (552°C) for 45 minutes. After soaking, turn the kiln off and let it cool to room temperature. Do not vent.

9. You are now ready to form your beautifully embossed bracelet. An embossed bracelet has several levels of thickness in the embossed design area. For this reason it must be heated and cooled more slowly and has a longer annealing soak time. Follow the same instructions as described for the single embossed medallion bracelet in step 12 on page 37.

Chapter 9 – Cane Bracelets

Tools & Equipment

- **Measuring & Preparation**
  steel ruler (inches & metric)
- **Safety:** 2 sets of kiln gloves & safety glasses
- **Fusing:** kiln with pyrometer, kiln shelf, flat-sided kiln posts 2" (5 cm), digital minute timer
- **Glass Cutting & Shaping:** glass cutter, breaking pliers, mosaic cutters, glass grinder, diamond blade glass saw
- **Forming & Manipulation:** bracelet forming mandrel, graphite forming tongs, two 12" (30 cm), tweezers, two 12" (30 cm) hemostat clamps, metal tray (cookie sheet)

Materials

- **Glass Supplies:** 4 pieces of glass rods in 4 assorted colors - 18" (45.7 cm) long, 4 pieces of glass rods, clear - 18" (45.7 cm) long, 1 piece of dichroic on clear thin glass (at least 3" x 4" (7.6 x 10.2 cm), glue (white craft) & applicator (toothpick)
- **Kiln Supplies:** kiln wash (hi-temp) & hake brush, pre-fired fiber paper - 1/32" (0.8 mm) thickness, Nichrome wire (or copper wire), 'boron nitride' based glass release

Glass canes are traditionally made using a hot glass furnace technique but this chapter will show you how to make a cane using an innovative fusing kiln technique. There are a couple of important details that I need to mention. First, you can't stretch and twist the cane bar by yourself, you will need a studio assistant to help you and that means you will need 2 sets of kiln gloves and safety glasses, one for you and one for your assistant. I need to point out that this is an advanced technique that will take some practice before you and your assistant get it just right. Your first few canes may not be perfect but the good news is they can often still be turned into unique bracelets, either cold worked and used as a whole or cut into components to add striking details to other designs. See Cane Restyling, chapter 11, page 58 & 59.

Cane Making Tools & Supplies:

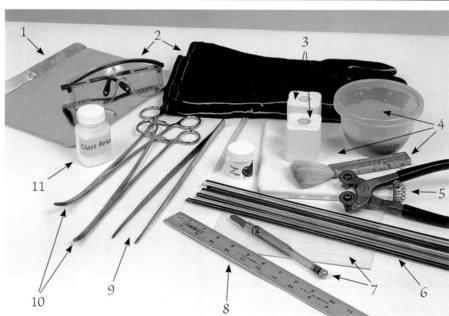

1. Metal Tray (cookie sheet)	6. Glass Rods, in Clear & Other Assorted Colors
2. Safety Glasses & Kiln Gloves	7. Glass Cutter & Fusing Glass
3. Flat-Sided Kiln Posts 2" (5 cm)	8. Steel Ruler (inches & metric)
4. Kiln Shelf, Kiln Wash (hi-temp) & Hake Brush	9. Tweezers 12" (30 cm)
5. Mosaic Tile Cutters	10. Hemostat Clamps 12" (30 cm)
	11. 'Boron Nitride' Based Glass Release

Jayne Persico presents...

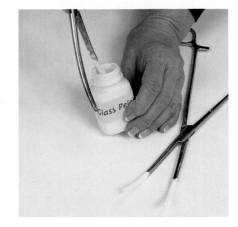

1. Prepare the kiln shelf with hi-temperature kiln wash. I use one part "Hi-Temp" kiln wash (a commercial product) to four parts cold water and apply the wash with a "hake" brush. When this first coat is dry (you can tell it's dry when the color has become pale) turn the shelf 90° and apply another coat of kiln wash in a cross direction. Apply 5 or 6 cross-alternating coats, always allowing sufficient time to dry between coats. When the shelf is completely dry, smooth out any brush stroke texture by rubbing the surface lightly with the dry tip of your finger.

2. Use the same "Hi-Temp" kiln wash mixture to put 3 or 4 coats on all surfaces of both kiln posts.

3. Dip the tips of both hemostat clamps into the glass release mixture and let it dry thoroughly. Important note: glass release is not the same as kiln wash. The 'boron nitride' based glass release that we're using here is a thick creamy mixture that will coat the tips of the hemostat clamps in a single dip. Be sure to keep the clamps open as the release is drying.

4. Use a mosaic tile cutter to cut the glass rods into 3" lengths. You will need 10 - 3" (7.6 cm) pieces of clear rods and 10 - 3" (7.6 cm) pieces of colored rods.

5. The next step is to put together four layers of rods using all 20 - 3" (7.6 cm) pieces. The color combination for 2 of the layers will be color-clear-color-clear-color and the combination for other 2 layers will be clear-color-clear-color-clear. This combination selection will encase the colors in clear, allowing light to pass through the cane and prevent the colors from bleeding together. The rods will be held together using a few dabs of white glue.

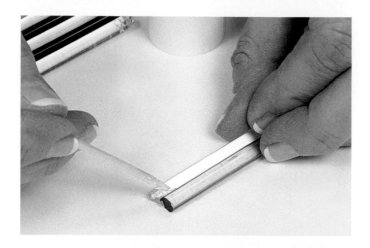

6. Place a piece of paper on your worktable and arrange the rod assemblies together sequentially on it (as shown on page 45). Then fasten each layer together by applying a dab of glue between each rod at the ends. Allow sufficient time for the glue to dry before trying to move these assemblies.

7. Measure the width of the rod assemblies and add 1/8" (3.2 mm) to the dimension of the widest set. Now cut 4 pieces of dichroic on clear thin glass, 3" (7.6 cm) long by the width you just calculated.

8. Set one of these dichroic glass pieces aside and divide the remaining 3 strips into 3 sections each. Be sure to keep each section together in the same sequence as they were cut apart.

9. The next step is to build the cane stack using the dichroic glass pieces and the rod assemblies. Setup the kiln base and place your prepared kiln shelf on the floor of the kiln. Lay the uncut 3" (7.6 cm) long dichroic glass strip on the kiln shelf with the DICHROIC SIDE DOWN. The dichroic coating will act as a separator, reducing the possibility of the fused bar sticking to the kiln shelf wash.

10. The next (second) layer will be one of the 5 glass rod units. Use one of the clear-color-clear-color-clear combinations.

11. The third layer will be one of the dichroic glass strips that you cut into 3 sections. Lay them on top of the glass rod layer in the same sequence as they were cut apart. These dichroic glass strips were cut into sections to give the trapped air a place to escape to minimize the incidence of air bubbles in the cane.

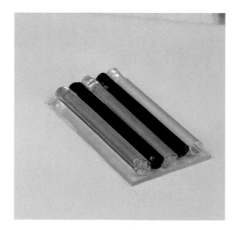

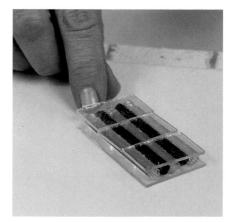

12. The fourth layer will be another one of the glass rod assemblies. This time we will use one of the color-clear-color-clear-color combinations.

13. The fifth layer will be another one of the dichroic glass strips, cut into 3 sections.

14. The sixth layer will be the other clear-color-clear-color-clear rod assembly.

15. The seventh layer will be another dichroic glass strip, cut into 3 sections.

16. The eighth (and final) layer will be the last remaining rod assembly; it should be a color-clear-color-clear-color combination.

17. Carefully place the prepared kiln posts on either side of the stack to act as a brace during the fusing process. Place the center ring on the kiln base and close the lid. Turn the kiln to the highest setting and set your timer for 30 minutes. The first stage of firing is to pre-fuse all the layers together. This should happen in the temperature range of 1375°F (746°C) to 1475°F (802°C). After 30 minutes, the kiln temperature should be above 1100°F (593°C) and that means you can safely open the kiln to view the firing. Wear gloves and safety glasses.

Tip: Be sure to locate your kiln on a table where you and your assistant can easily reach into the kiln from opposite sides. If you don't have a table that is narrow enough, position the kiln on the corner of your bench at a 45° angle. You and your assistant will have trouble-free access to reach in and clamp onto the fused bar at both ends.

Tip: Add more detail and color to your cane stack by placing stringers (thin glass 'strings') in the spaces between the rods. The fine intricate lines that stringers add to your cane can be quite stunning. Notice the use of a white stringers in the cane bracelet in the center of page 53.

Tip: It is always a good idea to keep an eye on a firing by opening the kiln for a peek but when making a kiln-cane it's crucial to catch the stack just as it is tacked fused together. If you let it go a little too long the stack can easily melt down and around the kiln posts. Making it difficult, if not impossible, to pull them out. So keep a close watch!

18. The stack is tacked together when it looks similar to the stack in the photo at left. If you don't feel the stack is fully tacked, close the lid and give it another few minutes to heat up, then check it again. When it's ready, turn off the kiln, remove the kiln lid set it aside and use the 12" (30 cm) tweezers to grasp and remove the kiln posts.

19. Place the hot kiln posts on a metal tray (i.e. cookie sheet) or other non-flammable surface and allow them to cool.

20. After the posts have been removed, the tacked stack should look similar to the photo below left (see tip at the top of this page).

21. Now replace the lid and turn the kiln to the highest setting. This second stage of firing will melt the stack into a fully fused multi colored mass that will flatten and spread out on the kiln shelf. The temperature range for full fusing in this small kiln is between 1450°F (788°C) to 1550°F (843°C). When the kiln reaches the optimum full fuse temperature for your kiln, turn the infinite switch down slightly to maintain this temperature and allow the stack to soak for another few minutes.

22. While the stack is fusing down it is important to gently move the glass on the shelf using the long tweezers to prevent it from sticking to the kiln shelf. Put on your gloves and glasses and use the 12" (30 cm) tweezers to reach into the kin (be sure to turn the kiln off momentarily while your reaching in, you could get a shock if you accidentally touch an element) and push on the glass until it moves slightly.

23. You should move the melted glass on the shelf for the first time just after removing the kiln posts. Move the glass again as it hits the full fuse temperature range, then move it again every minute or so during the fuse soak period (see step 21). The glass is ready to make into the cane when it has flattened and looks similar to the molten glass in the photo at right.

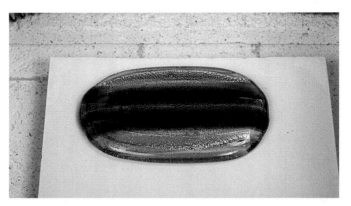

24. Now for the fun part. Have your studio assistant put on their gloves and glasses (put yours on as well if they are not on already) and each of you should have your hemostats ready. Stand across from your assistant with the kiln in between the two of you. Turn the kiln off, remove the kiln lid and set it aside. It is important that you and your assistant work in unison during these next few steps. Position the hemostat clamps approximately 1/2" (1.3 cm) in from the end of each side of the glass. Both of you need to clamp and lock the hemostats at the same time. Now together lift the glass and rest your hemostats on the edge of the kiln so that you are both holding the glass at the same level.

25. Now each of you should begin to twist the glass in a clockwise direction for several rotations. Since you are facing one another clockwise for each of you will result in a full twisting motion. Be sure to twist only at this point - do not pull yet! Try to create a pleasing spiral of mixed color, but don't over do it, this is one of those times when a little goes a long way.

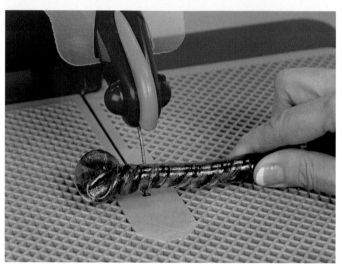

26. Now together with your assistant gently pull on the twisted glass. Stretch the cane until it is long enough to be used as a bracelet blank. Be careful that you don't pull it too far and make the cane so long it won't fit back into the kiln diagonally.

27. Have your assistant release the hemostat clamp at their end. Then use your clamp and tweezers to place the twisted cane back into the kiln diagonally on the shelf. Release and remove your hemostat clamp then quickly replace the kiln lid and turn the kiln controller to the anneal soak setting to maintain the annealing temperature for 45 minutes. After soaking, turn the kiln off and let it cool to room temperature. Do not vent.

28. Next we'll cold work the cane to get it ready to be formed into a bracelet blank. Use a rigid wire-type diamond blade glass saw (a Gemini Taurus 3 Ring Saw™ is shown in the photo) to cut the cane to the length of the bracelet calculation. Remember you will have to recalculate for dimension 'E' in the Measurement Data Form (on page 9) to take the thickness of the cane into account when determining this crucial measurement.

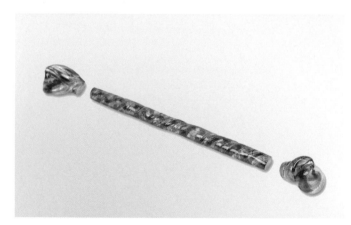

29. The photo at left shows the cane after both ends have been cut off.

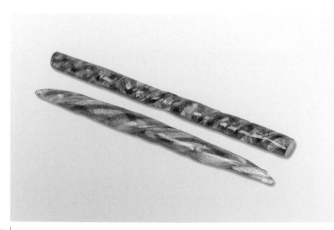

30. The bracelet will be more comfortable to wear and will have a more elegant look if the ends are tapered slightly. Use your glass grinder to create a taper about 1 1/2" (3.8 cm) in from each end. It is also a good idea to grind some glass away on the bottom surface to make it slightly flat. This will ensure the topside stays facing up during fire polishing and will help to steady the blank when it's balanced on the mandrel. This photo shows a cane before and after grinding.

31. After grinding, the blank must be placed back into the kiln to be 'fire polished' (see temperature chart on page 7). Remember to thoroughly clean the glass blank and place it on a prepared kiln shelf, being careful to not touch the surface with your fingers. When the edges appear to be glossy, the fire-polish is finished. Since this cane blank is thicker than the bracelet blanks we have done previously, adjust the kiln control switch for the optimum anneal temperature for your kiln, in the range of 960°F (516°C) to 1025°F (552°C) (see page 7 for details) and hold the anneal soak for 60 minutes. After soaking turn the kiln off and let it cool to room temperature. Do not vent.

32. When the bracelet is cool, it is ready to be formed. Due to the thickness of the cane the ramp up time to the forming temperature must be slower to prevent the bracelet from cracking due to thermal shock. Turn the kiln to the 'Low' setting for 8 minutes then turn it to the 'Medium' setting until the kiln has reached 900°F (482°C). You can now safely turn the kiln to the 'High' setting until the bracelet has reached the appropriate forming temperature in the range of 1250°F (677°C) to 1350°F (732°C).

33. Please review Chapter 4 on pages 18 to 21 for detailed instructions on bracelet forming. Remember that since this bracelet is thicker you should use a slower ramp up speed and a longer soak time prior to forming. Again due to the thickness, adjust the kiln controller for the optimum anneal temperature for your kiln, in the range of 960°F (516°C) to 1025°F (552°C) (see page 7 for details) and hold the anneal soak for 60 minutes. After soaking turn the kiln off and let it cool to room temperature. Do not vent.

Tip: One of the most rewarding aspects of making your own cane is the ability to control the amount of twist and the style of the sculptural effect that you can achieve. From loose twists to smooth spirals, each cane is a unique work of art. As you gain experience, you will begin to develop your cane with individual characteristics that may eventually evolve into your own signature style.

Bracelet Showcase Gallery

Chapter 10 - Making Your Own Murrini Rods

Tools & Equipment

- **Safety:** kiln gloves & safety glasses
- **Fusing:** kiln with pyrometer, kiln shelf, flat-sided kiln posts 2" (5 cm), digital minute timer
- **Glass Cutting & Shaping:** glass cutter, breaking pliers, mosaic cutters, glass grinder, diamond blade glass saw
- **Forming & Manipulation:** bracelet forming mandrel, graphite forming tongs, two 12" (30 cm), tweezers, two 12" (30 cm) hemostat clamps, Murrini maker (mullite mold), metal tray (cookie sheet)

Materials

- **Glass Supplies:**
  For Murrini Rods: piece of clear thin glass, assorted pieces of colored glass (standard & thin), assorted colors of stringers &/or noodles (optional)
  For Cane Stack: piece of dichroic on clear thin glass, glue (white craft) & applicator (toothpick)
- **Kiln Supplies:** kiln wash (hi-temp) & hake brush, pre-fired fiber paper - 1/32" (0.8 mm) thickness, Nichrome wire (or copper wire), 'boron nitride' based glass release

In the previous chapter we created the pattern bar for the cane bracelet using commercially produced glass rods. However, it's easy to create you're own glass rods by cutting thin strips of compatible glass and fusing them in a Murrini Maker. The many advantages include the ability to; create colored rods that may not be available, create rods that have a COE compatibility with other fusing glass in your collection, create bars that use up scrap glass or bars that have different colors along their length. A major advantage for us is the ability to make our own filigrana rods. These are rods that consist of a color core encased in clear glass. This will eliminate the need to separate the color rods with clear rods as we did in the previous chapter.

1. A Murrini Maker is similar to a kiln shelf however it has parallel slots molded into the top surface where the glass is placed and fused to form a Murrini rod. It must be prepared in the same way as a kiln shelf, with 5 or 6 coats of hi-temperature kiln wash. Follow the shelf preparation step in Chapter 9, step 1 on page 45. When the Murrini Maker is completely dry, smooth out any brush stroke texture by running the tip of your finger (or a soft artists brush) along and through the slots.

Jayne Persico presents...

2. This photo shows a side view of the Murrini Maker, loaded and ready to fire. Notice the unique layering in the first 3 slots to create a special type of rod known as filigrana. The bottom, top and both sides are thin clear compatible glass. The center 'core' glass is a colored compatible glass strip from either thick or thin glass. This is also an excellent time to use stringers or noodles to make the color threads finer and more intricate. The fourth slot is setup to make a dichroic rod. The bottom layer is thin compatible dichroic glass (dichroic side down) and the top layer is a thick strip of a colored compatible glass. You should also notice that the slots are not all the same width, allowing you to create several different widths of rods and color combinations in the same firing.

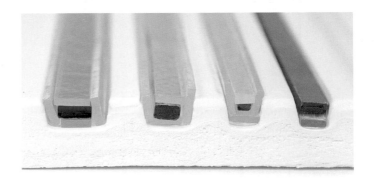

3. This photo (at right) is a top view of the Murrini Maker loaded, set in the kiln and ready to be fired. Close the lid and turn the kiln to the 'Medium' setting until it has reached 1000°F (538°C). This slower ramp up speed is to give the Murrini Maker time to heat up. If this ceramic mold is heated too fast it could crack or completely break apart.

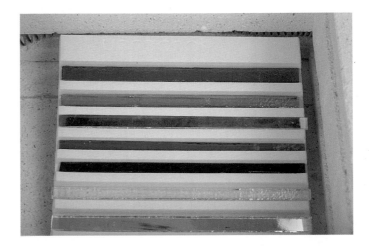

4. When the kiln temperature is approaching the full fuse range of 1450°F (788°C) to 1550°F (843°C) (see page 7 for temperature details) put your kiln gloves and safety glasses on and open the lid to check the progress. The rods are fully fused when the tops are slightly rounded and have a glossy appearance. If it needs more time, close the lid and check again in 5 or so minutes. When you are satisfied that the rods are fused, simply turn the kiln off and let it cool to room temperature. Do not vent. The rods are small enough that it is not necessary to cycle them through an anneal soak.

5. Now we will create the color stack using the rods that we made in the Murrini Maker. In chapter 9 we used 5 commercial rods per layer and had 8 layers in total. The filigrana rods we've made are thicker and are encased in clear and that means we will only need three rods per layer plus we can make the bar with only 6 layers (3 layers of clear dichroic thin glass and 3 layers of the filigrana rods). Use a mosaic cutter to cut your filigrana rods into 3" (7.6 cm) lengths. You will need a total of 9 pieces of colored filigrana rods.

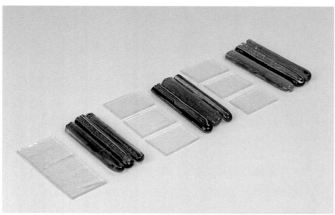

6. Place a piece of paper on your worktable and arrange the filigrana rods sequentially, in 3 sets of 3 together on it. Now fasten each layer together by applying a dab of glue between each rod at the ends. Allow sufficient time for the glue to dry before moving these assemblies.

7. Measure the width of the rod assemblies and add 1/8" (3.2 mm) to the dimension of the widest set. Now cut 4 pieces of dichroic on clear thin glass, 3" long by the width you just calculated. Set one of these dichroic glass strips aside and divide the remaining 2 strips into 3 sections each. Be sure to keep each section together in the same sequence as they were cut apart.

8. Build the cane stack using the dichroic glass pieces and the filigrana rod assemblies that you have prepared. Setup the kiln base and place a prepared kiln shelf on the floor of the kiln. Lay the uncut 3" long (7.6 cm) dichroic glass strip on the kiln shelf with the DICHROIC SIDE DOWN. The dichroic coating will act as a separator, reducing the possibility of the fused bar sticking to the kiln shelf wash.

9. The next (second) layer will be one of the filigrana rod assemblies. The third layer will be one of the dichroic glass strips that you cut into 3 sections. Lay them on top of the glass rod layer in the same sequence as they were cut apart (this is the same process as step 9 to 13 on page 46 & 47). The fourth layer will be another one of the filigrana rod assemblies. The fifth layer will be another one of the dichroic glass strips, cut into 3 sections. The sixth (and final) layer will be the last filigrana rod assembly.

10. Place the kiln washed kiln posts on either side of the stack to act as a brace during the fusing process. The photo at left shows a side view of the cane stack supported by kiln posts. Place the center ring on the kiln base and close the lid. Turn the kiln to the highest setting and set your timer for 30 minutes. The first stage of firing is to pre-fuse all the layers together. This should happen in the temperature range of 1375°F (746°C) to 1475°F (802°C). After 30 minutes, the kiln temperature should be above 1100°F (593°C) and that means you can safely open the kiln to view the firing.

Jayne Persico presents...

11. Follow the tack fuse and full fuse instructions in Chapter 9, steps 18 to 23 on page 48 & 49.

12. The glass is ready to be twisted and pulled into a cane when it looks similar to the multi colored molten glass in the photos above. Have your studio assistant stand across from you with the kiln in between. Turn the kiln off, remove the lid and set it aside. Position the hemostat clamps approximately 1/2" (1.3 cm) in from the end of each side of the glass and lock the hemostats at the same time.

13. Lift and twist the cane by following the complete cane making instructions described in Chapter 9, steps 24 to 27 on page 49 & 50. This photo shows the cane after it has been twisted and pulled, ready to be placed back into the kiln for annealing and cool down.

14. The photo at right shows the 3 stages of a cane in the process of becoming a bracelet. From left to right; twisted and pulled, tapered and ground (cold worked) and fire polished. Be sure to review these steps in Chapter 9, steps 28 to 31 on page 50 & 51. The final process is to form the cane blank into a bracelet, follow the steps in Chapter 4 on page 18 to 21. Remember that since this bracelet is thicker you should use a slower ramp up speed, a longer soak time prior to forming and an anneal soak of 60 minutes at the optimum anneal temperature for your kiln (see page 7 for details).

Chapter 11 - Cane Restyling

One of the wonderful aspects of glass fusing is the opportunity to create exquisite art using components left over from past projects. And some of the most useful components come from bits and pieces of cane. Sometimes all that is required is a hole to be drilled or some strategic wire wrapping to create a pendant. Other times a small piece of a cane be fused 'jewel-like' onto a blank. This chapter will explore some of these possibilities to get you thinking about creative ways you can utilize the valuable components in your 'leftovers' bin.

This is a quick and easy way to create a pendant that is a perfect match for a bracelet. Transform the cutoff ends of a cane into wonderful free-formed pendants. Simply drill an opening at one end to accommodate a necklace bail and fire polish. Or you could encase the cutoff end using gold or silver wire wrapping techniques. This photo shows 3 examples of cane-end pendants.

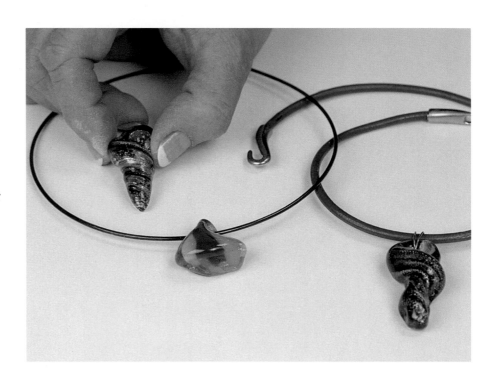

At first glance you might not recognize this spectacular bracelet as a cane bracelet - but it is! The cane didn't turn out quite the way I wanted it to be, so I full fused it onto a base blank of dichroic on black glass. The glass fused down nicely producing a pleasing mix of colors with a shiny smooth top surface. After cooling I did some cold working on my grinder to create the shape and size I wanted then I put it back into the kiln to fire polish. It was then finished with one last firing, to shape it over the bracelet mandrel.

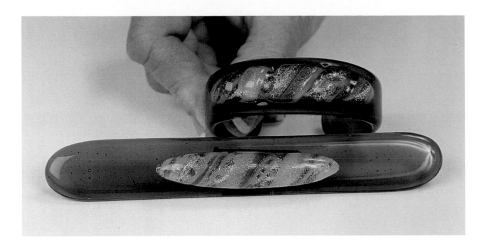

You can create an interesting effect by tack-fusing a small piece of cane onto the center of a bracelet blank. This bracelet was made by first full fusing the medium blue bracelet blank then tack fusing a small piece of cane (that was pre-shaped, cold-worked and fire polished) onto the surface. The bracelet was formed in the usual manner.

This interesting 'wrapped candy' bracelet was created in several steps. First the appliqué design was made from a piece of cane that was heated to full fuse temperature. The cooled piece was then cold-worked to shape the fish tail ends. Then it was heated to forming temperature and tweezers were used to pinch-in the 2 neck areas. Finally a 2 layer black and dichroic bracelet blank was created and the candy appliqué was tack fused to the surface. The bracelet was formed in the usual manner.

This cane bracelet was formed from a cane made in the usual manner. The cooled cane was cold-worked and sized then it was placed back into the kiln and heated to forming temperature. The neck areas were created using tweezers to pinch-in the hot glass to compose a pleasing pattern. The bracelet was formed in the usual manner.

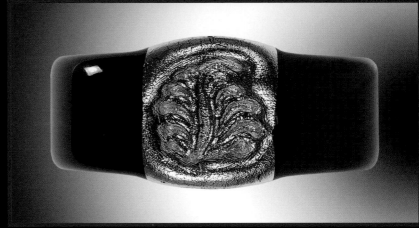

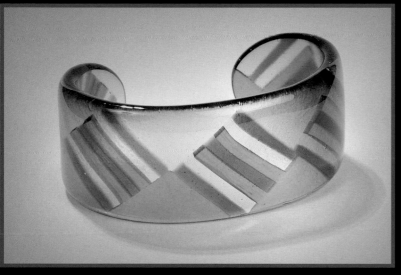

Chapter 12 – Pattern Bar Bracelets

A glass pattern bar is nothing more than a block of differently colored glass pieces that have been arranged and fused together to form a pattern that runs all the way through the glass lengthwise. Slices are then cut off the end of a pattern bar to create design tiles that can be fused into other projects.

Tools & Equipment
- **Measuring & Preparation**
  steel ruler (inches & metric), marking pen (fine point)
- **Safety:** kiln gloves & glasses
- **Fusing:** kiln with pyrometer, kiln shelf, minute timer
- **Glass Cutting & Shaping:**
  glass cutter, breaking pliers, glass grinder, diamond blade glass saw
- **Forming & Manipulation:**
  bracelet forming mandrel, graphite forming tongs, damming walls (kiln shelves, mullite board, or fiberboard), flat-sided kiln posts 2" (5 cm) (to support the walls), metal tray (cookie sheet)

Materials
- **Glass Supplies:** assorted colors of fusing glass - standard thickness, glue (white craft) & applicator (toothpick)
- **Kiln Supplies:** pre-fired fiber paper - 1/32" (0.8 mm) thickness, Thinfire™ paper, Nichrome wire (or copper wire)

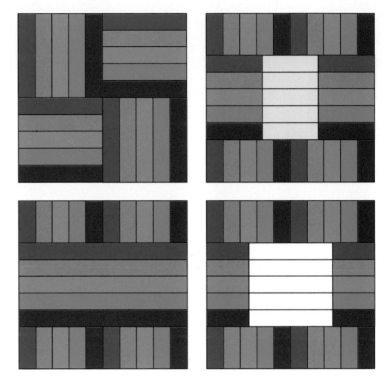

These pattern bar variations show the profile end of a pattern bar and are reproduced here in actual size. The colors and layout combination could be any fusing compatible glass of your choosing.

Creating A Pattern Bar:

1. Cut 20 strips of assorted colors of compatible glass 4" long by 1/2" wide (10.2 x 1.3 cm). Divide the 20 strips of glass into four groups and lay out a color scheme (using your glass choices) similar to the example in this photo at right.

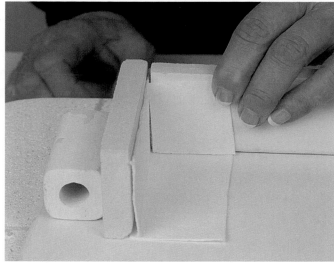

2. The photo above shows the end view of our pattern bar stack. This design configuration is shown in the top left corner of the illustration on the previous page. The other 3 design configurations would require glass strip widths from 1/4" (1.3 cm) to 1" (2.5 cm). Glue each 5 piece stack (on the ends only) to make loading the assembly into the kiln easier.

3. The next step is to setup a dam for the pattern bar assembly. You will need the fiber paper, 4 damming walls, 4 kiln posts and a kiln shelf. Setup the kiln base and place the kiln shelf on the floor of the kiln, then place a sheet of fiber paper on the shelf. Setup two sides of the dam using kiln posts to supporting the walls. Line both of these walls with fiber paper.

4. Carefully position the glass stack against the first two walls of the dam. Now add the 3rd and 4th walls by first placing a sheet of fiber paper between the glass and the wall then support these walls with kiln posts.

5. Now we're ready to fire the kiln to fully fuse the glass stack into a solid glass pattern bar. Place the center ring on the base and close the lid. Turn the kiln to the highest setting and set your timer for 30 minutes. Ramp the kiln up to full fusing temperature between 1450°F (788°C) to 1550°F (843°C) or to the optimum fusing temperature for your particular kiln. When the kiln has reached the desired fusing temperature adjust the controller to soak the pattern bar at this temperature until it is fully fused. This could take anywhere from 10-20 additional minutes from when you began the fuse soak. Visually monitor the progress until you determine that the bar is fully fused. Vent the kiln down to the anneal soak temperature, set the control switch to the anneal setting and allow it to soak for 90 minutes. After soaking turn the kiln off and let it cool to room temperature. Do not vent.

6. Disassemble the kiln and set the lid and center ring aside. Remove the kiln posts, the damming walls and the fiber paper. Your pattern bar should look like the one in the photo at right.

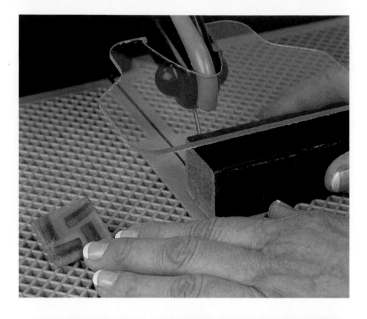

7. Now we'll cut some slices from the end of the pattern bar using a diamond blade glass saw. You want the slices to be approximately the same thickness as standard fusing glass (approximately 1/8" (3.2 mm). If you have one of the 'slicer' attachments for your saw this would be a great opportunity to use it.

8. The photo below left shows what a pattern bar slice looks like. Notice how the pattern is very similar to the design in the illustration on page 60.

9. We will make a bracelet blank using 3 of the pattern bar slices and 4 pieces of a coordinating color, cut to fit in between the slices and to cap off both ends. Remember to measure and cut these components to make the resulting assembly the size of dimension 'E' in your Bracelet Data Form (page 9). Setup the kiln base and place a prepared kiln shelf on the floor of the kiln. Lay the base layer assembly on the kiln shelf as shown below left.

10. The top layer of the bracelet is a standard thickness of compatible clear glass. This glass needs to be slightly larger in length and width (see Chapter 2, step 2 on page 12). Clean this glass and place it on top of the base layer.

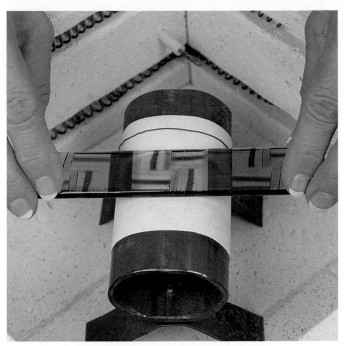

11. Fuse the blank. Then grind size and fire polish it by following the instructions in Chapter 2 on pages 13 to 14. This photo shows what the full fused pattern bar bracelet blank should look like after cold working and fire polishing.

12. Form the bracelet as instructed in chapter 3 and 4 on pages 15 to 21. Note: If the pattern bar slices were thick - 1/4" (6.4 mm) or more, it would be a good idea to increase the anneal soak time from 30 minutes to 45 minutes.

13. When the bracelet has cooled to room temperature, remove it from the mandrel.

14. The photo below right shows the finished pattern bar bracelet. It only took 3 slices to make this bracelet and a 4" pattern bar should yield at least 20 good slices. So you have lots of experimenting to do.

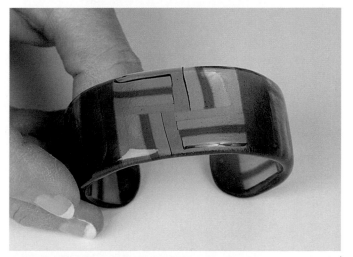

Jayne Persico pres

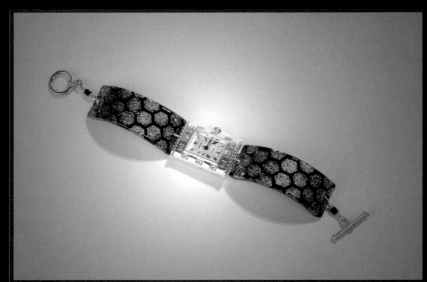

Chapter 13 - Glass Watchbands

Tools & Equipment

- **Measuring & Preparation** steel ruler (inches & metric)
- **Safety:** kiln gloves & glasses
- **Fusing:** kiln with pyrometer, kiln shelf, minute timer
- **Glass Cutting & Shaping:** glass cutter, breaking pliers, glass grinder, high-speed drill with 5/64" (2 mm) hollow-core bit, plastic container with micro foam sheet
- **Forming & Manipulation:** bracelet forming mandrel
- **Jeweler's Tools:** flush cutters (wire cutters), needle nosed pliers, round nosed pliers, watch-pin tool, metal skewers - 3/64" (1.2 mm)

Materials

- **Glass Supplies:** black fusing glass - thin (large enough for 2 watch band components), dichroic patterned clear fusing glass - thin (large enough for 2 watch band components), glue (white craft) & applicator (toothpick)
- **Jewelry Supplies:** glass seed-beads - size 8/0 (3 mm), bar and loop clasp findings, 4' (1.2m) length of 21 gauge round, half-hard wire (sterling silver wire or gold wire), watch face with standard double connection points
- **Kiln Supplies:** kiln wash (hi-temp) & hake brush, pre-fired fiber paper - 1/32" (0.8 mm) thickness, Nichrome wire (or copper wire)

I have been making these curved glass watchbands from the very beginning of the development of this kiln formed bracelet process and their popularity has remained extraordinary. I think it's because a glass watchband is such an unusual way to dress up an otherwise quite common accessory - the wristwatch. The design possibilities are remarkable if you consider the various shapes you could use for the components such as rectangle, triangle, semi-oval, half-octagon, to name just a few (hint; use the watch face shape for inspiration). Add to this the vast array of fusing colors, dichroic patterns, pattern bars, plus other surface decoration techniques (e.g. wire wrapping with beads) the imagination runs wild!

1. The size of the glass watchband components is not as critical as it is when creating one-piece bracelets in the previous chapters. The reason for this is the size can be fine-tuned when we're wire wrapping the clasp mechanism. The main consideration for determining the length and width of the glass components is the style of the watch face.

The width of the band should be somewhere between the length of the watch pin and the width of the watch face. The length of the glass component varies from 2" to 2 1/4" (5.1 to 5.7 cm). Basically, if the watch face is small, the length needs be closer to the longer dimension to compensate, if the watch face is large, the length is should be more toward the shorter dimension.

2. I recommend using 2 layers of thin fusible glass for watchbands. Fused components made from thin glass are lighter weight, resulting in a more comfortable fit (as compared to a band made from standard thickness glass). For this project I have selected a thin black glass for the base layer and a thin clear patterned dichroic glass for the top layer. Cut the components to the shape and size that you determined based on the watch face that you will use.

3. Setup the kiln base and place the prepared kiln shelf on the floor of the kiln. Stack the glass components on the shelf, place the center ring on the base and close the lid. Turn the kiln to the highest setting and set your timer for 30 minutes. Allow the kiln to ramp up to the full fuse temperature range of 1450°F (788°C) to 1550°F (843°C) or to the optimum fusing temperature that you have determined for your particular kiln. These blanks are made using 2 layers of thin glass so it is even more important to monitor the progress closely from 1425°F (774°C) until it is finished. When you are satisfied that the blank has reached full fuse, turn the kiln off and let it cool to room temperature. Do not open the door or vent the kiln during cool down.

4. The next step is to drill holes in both ends of the components to accommodate the wire wrapping. Line a shallow plastic container with a piece of micro foam sheet and enough cold water to cover the foam to a depth of about 3/8" (1 cm). Lay the glass component on top of the foam, front side up. Make sure the glass is completely under water so both it and the diamond bit will maintain a cool temperature during the drilling. Push down firmly on the glass with your fingers. The foam will help you to hold the glass securely while drilling. Use a high-speed drill (e.g. Dremel™) with a 5/64" (2 mm) hollow core diamond drill bit to drill the required holes. Always use the highest speed setting on the drill (at least 20,000 RPM).

Tip: When drilling with a Dremel™ tool it is not necessary to apply downward pressure on the glass. The weight of the drill itself will be sufficient to cut through the glass. Patience will be your greatest helper while drilling. All you have to do is hold the drill bit in that same spot, without pressing down and let the high speed Dremel™ drill do all the work.

Special note: A standard drill has speeds much slower than a Dremel™ drill and will not work satisfactorily to drill holes. Due to the slower speed, if you try to use a hollow core diamond bit in a standard drill the diamond coating will fatigue quickly and ruin the bit.

5. After drilling, the components need to be fire polished. Place them on a prepared kiln shelf and turn the kiln to the 'High' setting until it reaches the fire polishing temperature range of 1325°F (718°C) to 1425°F (774°C). When the edges are glossy, turn the kiln off and allow it to cool. Caution: Do not allow the glass to get too hot or to soak at the fire polishing temperature for too long as you'll run the risk of closing over the holes that you just drilled.

6. Watchband components are always formed on the medium mandrel. Loosen the screws on the legs of the mandrel and turn the legs 90° to allow the mandrel to lay on its side, on the kiln shelf . The mandrel needs to be on its side to ensure the watchband components are shaped correctly to the outside oval of the mandrel.

7. Setup the kiln base and place the mandrel on its side directly on the kiln floor. Lay a piece of pre-fired 1/32" (0.8 mm) fiber paper on the top surface of the mandrel. The fiber paper can be secured with wire if you choose but it is not necessary for this process because the paper is soft and will stay in place on its own. Place the components on the mandrel and adjust them until they are centered, balanced and perpendicular to the mandrel (see Chapter 4, step 2 page 18 for more details).

8. Place the center ring on the kiln base and close the lid. Turn the kiln to 'High' and set your timer for 10 minutes. The instant the kiln reaches 1100°F (593°C) begin to visually monitor the slump. When the glass begins to bend, turn the kiln down to maintain this temperature until the components are completely slumped. Allowing the temperature to go higher will slump the glass faster but there is an increased risk of closing over the holes that you drilled. When the components are fully slumped, turn the kiln off and allow it to cool to room temperature. An anneal soak will not be necessary since these components are relatively small.

Jayne Persico presents...

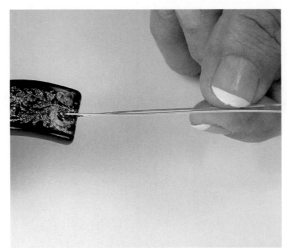

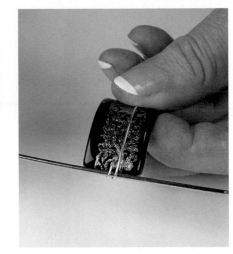

9. The watch components are now ready to be attached to the watch face movement. You will need approximately 2' (61 cm) of 21 gauge, sterling silver or gold filled, half-hard, round wire to complete one watch.

10. Cut a 7" (18 cm) length of wire. Slide one of the watchband components onto the wire and center it. Bend both the front and back wires up until they are parallel to one another.

11. Place a 3/64" (1.2 mm) diameter metal rod (I use a metal skewer used for cooking) between the wires and move it until it is resting directly on the glass. Be careful you do not cross the wires over the glass prior to placing the skewer. Wrap the wire that is behind the skewer toward you one turn around the skewer. Then wrap the front wire away from you one turn around the skewer.

12. Continue to coil the wire around the mandrel making certain that the coil has an equal amount of turns on either side.

13. After a few coil wraps use the needle nosed pliers to crimp and compress the coils on the front side of skewer and squeeze them together into one tight unit. Move the pliers to the back of the skewer and repeat.

14. This coil is going to house the watch pin that will connect the band to the watch itself. This means the coil needs to be fit into the space between the watch pin tabs on the watch face. Check the coil width against the watch face (or the pins). Finish by compressing it one more time before removing the metal rod. Repeat this same coiling procedure on the other watchband component.

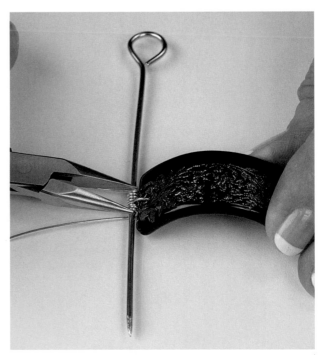

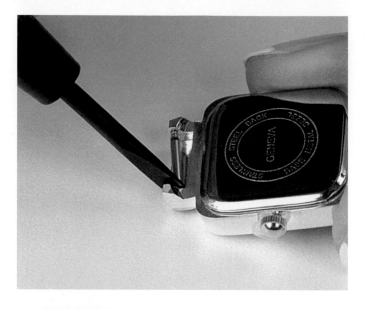

15. The components may need to be adjusted to fit into the watch face correctly. For a final fitting, turn the watch face upside down, remove the pins and set them aside.

16. Try fitting the coil unit into the watch. If it is too long simply clip an equal amount of the coil from either end using the tip of your flush cutters.

17. Attach the watch component to the watch face by inserting the pin through the coil then use the watch tool to secure the pin to the watch pin tabs on the watch face.

18. Attach both glass watchband components to the watch face. The next step is to create the closure clasp assembly.

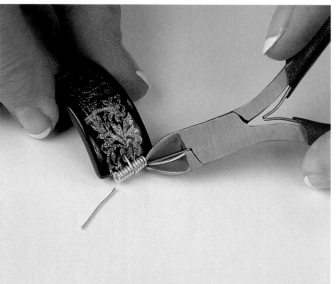

Tip: To give the watch a designer's touch use a watch face that has a housing to hide the pin loop. You can see this housing under the pin in the photo at top but if you look carefully at all the watches on pages 66 & 67 you will not see an exposed pin loop because they are all hidden under a built-in covering.

19. Cut a 4" (10.2 cm) length of the wire you're using. Use the needle nosed pliers to put a 90° bend in the wire approximately 1 1/2" (3.8 cm) down from one end.

20. Now use the round nose pliers and insert the bent wire into the jaw so that one end of the wire is pointing down (at the 6 o'clock position) and the other end is to the right (at the 3 o'clock position).

Note: These wire wrapping instructions, the positions, descriptions and directions are written from the workers point of view. However the photos were taken as the work would appear if you were looking at someone else's work.

21. Hold the pliers in your left hand and grasp the wire at the three o'clock position with your right and bend it up and over the top jaw of the pliers to the 9 o'clock position, thus forming the first part of the loop.

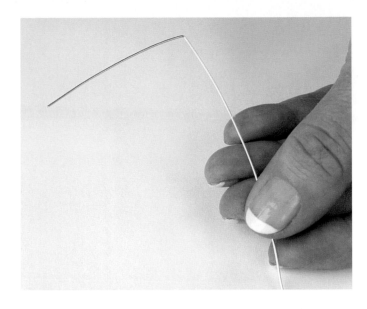

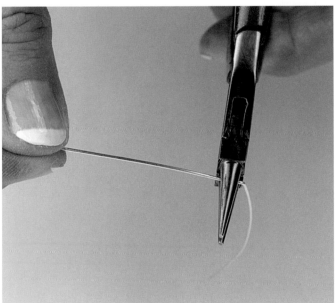

Tip: This loop must be large enough to accommodate the thickness of the glass component so that it has free movement. The size of the loop is determined by the position of the wire on the round nose pliers, thus the further back in the jaw the larger the loop and vise-versa. Take this into account when placing the wire.

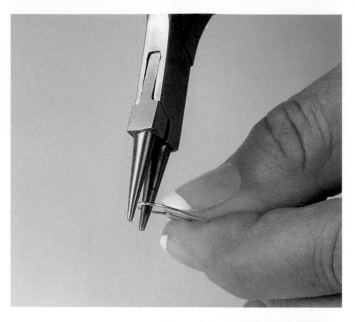

22. Now slide the wire off the upper jaw of the round nose pliers, move it down to the lower jaw and slide it back on.

23. Continue to wrap the wire down and around the lower jaw until it has reached back to the 3 o'clock position (from your point of view).

24. Remove the wire from the pliers. Your loop should look like the one in this photo.

25. Thread one of the glass components onto the wire and into the loop. (It doesn't matter if you insert it from the back or the front.)

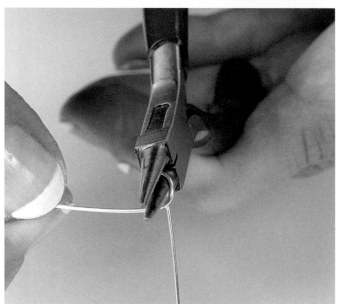

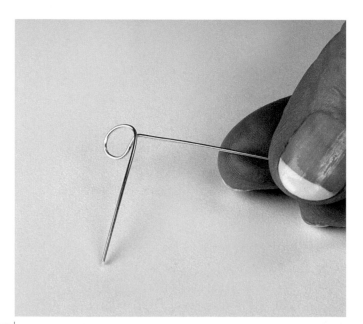

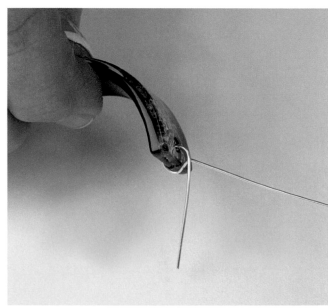

26. Grasp the wire loop as shown, with the tip of the round nose pliers tight against the glass.

27. Close off the loop by wrapping the shorter end of the wire around the longer end. Wrap it tightly for 2 revolutions. This will form a small coil wrap. Clip the excess wire from the wrap end with your wire cutters and crimp it neatly with your needle nose pliers.

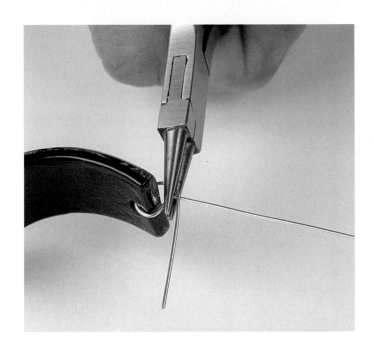

28. Place the watch on your wrist and measure the opening on the inside of your wrist. This is to determine how many beads should be added to make the watch fit correctly. The opening in the photo is approximately. 1 1/2" (3.8 cm). This measurement will require two beads (one on each end) to size this watch correctly. A bead adds approximately 1/4" (6.4 mm) to each end of the band or 1/2" (1.3 cm) total. This means you can add more beads to increase the length or eliminate them to tighten the band.

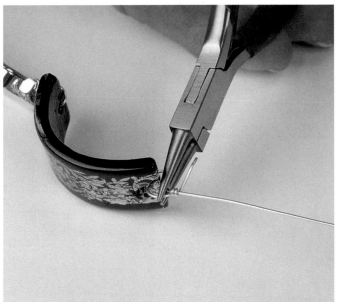

Note About Size & Fit: This watch is not designed to fit snugly to your arm in the same way a traditional wristwatch might. The fit is much looser and is comparable to a bracelet fit. A certain amount of slack is required to enable you to comfortably pull the toggle bar through the loop.

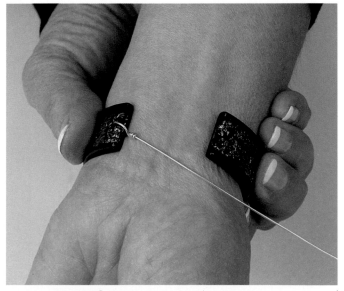

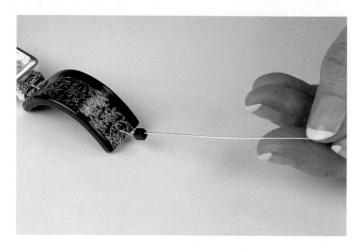

29. Thread one glass bead onto the wire.

30. Now we are going to form another loop using the same technique as in the previous steps. This loop needs to be much smaller because it will be used to attach to the "bar & loop" findings (also known as a toggle clasp). To make a small loop, grasp the extending wire with the very tip of your round nose pliers tight against the bead. Bend the wire back to put a 90° bend in the wire.

31. Remove the pliers and reposition them by placing the tips of the pliers above this 90° bend (photo at bottom left). The bead should be pointing down, while the "wire only" end should be pointing to the 3 o'clock position.

32. Grasp the end of the wire (at the 3 o'clock position) with your left hand and bend the wire up and over the top jaw of the pliers to the 9 o'clock position to form the first part of the loop. It should look like the wire in the photo above.

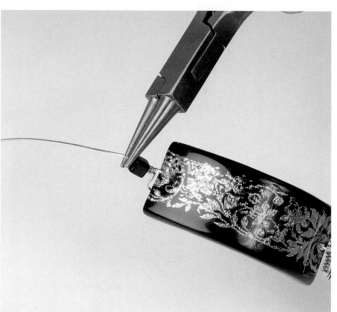

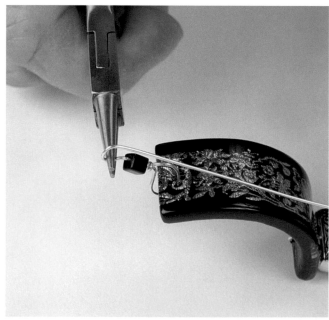

33. Slide the wire off the upper jaw of the round nose pliers, move it down to the lower jaw and slide it back on, still at the tip (see photo above right). Now continue to wrap the wire down and around the lower jaw until it has reached back to the 3 o'clock position. You'll now have a complete loop.

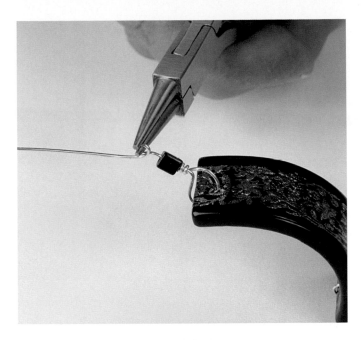

34. Thread one of the clasp parts onto this loop wire. The toggle or bar part of the clasp should be on the 6 o'clock end of the watchband and the loop part of the clasp should be on the 12 o'clock side of the watchband. Grasp the wire loop tight against the finding with the tip of the round nose pliers. Close off the loop by wrapping the wire two revolutions toward the bead.

35. This will form another small coil wrap. Clip excess wire with your flush cutters and crimp it neatly with your needle nose pliers. Don't forget to crimp this securely so that it will not scratch the wearer, snag clothing or begin to "unravel".

36. You have now completed one side of your watchband. Repeat steps 18 to 34 to attach the clasp to the glass component on the other half of your watchband.

Bracelet Showcase Gallery

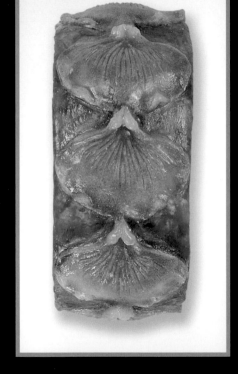

Index

Wardell
PUBLICATIONS INC

Instruction, Inspiration and Innovation for the Art Glass Communnity

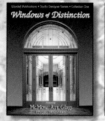

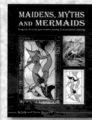

e-mail: info@wardellpublications.com   website: www.wardellpublications.com